Praise for *Married and Still Loving It*

Who knew marriage could get better with age? Gary Chapman and Harold Myra give us a high-def picture of the realities of marriage in the second half of life, but they also show the joy, hope, humor, and *life* that a mature relationship provides. A welcome message!

—**Marshall Shelley**, senior editor, *Christianity Today*

My bookshelves are filled with marriage advice, but not one is so specific and helpful for the second half of marriage as *Married and Still Loving It*. Marriages don't survive on cruise control. They require intentionality and wisdom in *every stage*. This book is practical, easy-to-read, and will navigate you through real-life challenges to a marriage that is aging well.

—**Juli Slattery**, president and cofounder, Authentic Intimacy

All too often the Old Testament tells us about smart, high-achieving people who did well for decades (Noah, Solomon, Joash, Hezekiah, Josiah), only to derail in their later years. Here in our own time, the alarming rise in silver-haired divorces troubles us all. If you want to buck that trend, this is the book you need. Read, learn, and find the keys to finishing strong.

—**Dean Merrill**, publisher and award-winning author who's been married fifty years

A deep and encouraging book!!

—**Jay Kesler**, president emeritus, Taylor University

MARRIED AND STILL LOVING IT

The Joys and Challenges of the Second Half

GARY CHAPMAN
HAROLD MYRA

MOODY PUBLISHERS
CHICAGO

Edited by Elizabeth Cody Newenhuyse
Interior design: Ragont Design
Cover design: Dean Renninger
Cover photo of hiking couple copyright © 2015 by Robin Skjoldborg/Getty Images (575619315). All rights reserved.
Chapman cover photo: P.S. Photography
Photo of Joni and Ken Tada used by permission of Joni Eareckson Tada of Joni and Friends.

Library of Congress Cataloging-in-Publication Data

Names: Chapman, Gary D., author. | Myra, Harold Lawrence, author.
Title: Married and still loving it : the joys and challenges of the second half / Gary Chapman, Harold Myra.
Description: Chicago, IL : Moody Publishers, [2016] | Includes bibliographical references.
Identifiers: LCCN 2015035335 | ISBN 9780802412928
Subjects: LCSH: Married people—Religious life. | Older couples—Religious life. | Man-woman relationships—Religious aspects—Christianity. | Marriage--Religious aspects—Christianity. | Marital quality.
Classification: LCC BV4596.M3 C4835 2016 | DDC 248.8/44—dc23 LC record available at http://lccn.loc.gov/2015035335

We hope you enjoy this book from Moody Publishers. Our goal is to provide high-quality, thought-provoking books and products that connect truth to your real needs and challenges. For more information on other books and products written and produced from a biblical perspective, go to www.moodypublishers.com or write to:

Moody Publishers
820 N. LaSalle Boulevard
Chicago, IL 60610

1 3 5 7 9 10 8 6 4 2

Printed in the United States of America

To our wives, Karolyn Chapman and Jeanette Myra,
with whom we are sharing the joys and
challenges of the second half;
and to the many couples who told us their
stories of resilience, faith, and love.

Contents

Introduction

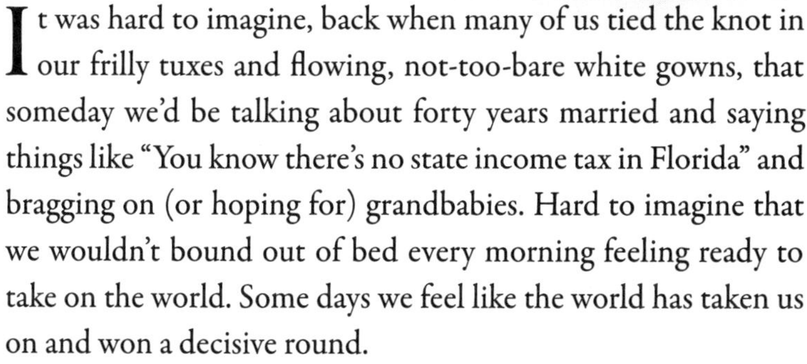

Love in the "Beautiful Season"

It was hard to imagine, back when many of us tied the knot in our frilly tuxes and flowing, not-too-bare white gowns, that someday we'd be talking about forty years married and saying things like "You know there's no state income tax in Florida" and bragging on (or hoping for) grandbabies. Hard to imagine that we wouldn't bound out of bed every morning feeling ready to take on the world. Some days we feel like the world has taken us on and won a decisive round.

But here we are.

Is the second half the "best half"? Some studies say yes. Research shows that people are generally happier as they age. But beyond the studies, what does it really *feel* like to be a married boomer going through sometimes-wrenching life changes? Listen to a good friend of ours:

> *I was really hit with the idea of growing older together when my husband and I were sitting in the waiting room of*

our local eye clinic, a world-class facility. People come from all over to be treated. They all appeared to be older than we, which felt so refreshing. Some had walkers. Others wore dark glasses. While one couple talked animatedly with each other, another couple was on their screens just like young folks. Other couples were literally holding each other up. Just sitting in the waiting room made me ask, "Is this us in a few years? What does this future look like, growing old with my husband?"

What does it look like to thrive in our marriages in our fifties, sixties, and beyond? Yes, the mature years can often be happier as we know ourselves better and are perhaps more at peace with our lives. Marriage in the empty-nest stage can be a time of companionship and contentment. Yet we can't ignore the realities of health limitations, worries about money, and the prospects for our grown children. We may be lonely as friends move away. Some of us are watching parents fade into dementia. Others are still getting kids through college, or wondering about the next stage of their work lives. The wisdom of aging sometimes looks more like an admission of how much you *don't* know.

So again, how does all this work?

We know the prescriptions for building a strong marriage: communication, mutual respect, making time for each other, and healthy approaches to conflict. I (Gary) have been privileged to counsel and speak to couples on these issues for years. But seasoned couples also have a wealth of wisdom and experience to bring to bear on these challenges. So along with practical insights about navigating this "second half," we are sharing the stories of husbands and wives who are wrestling with the realities of this season.

As we talked with these couples, we repeatedly found a paradox: happiness tempered by sober awareness of the realities of life. Some were positive, and we got caught up in their laughter. Yet some conversations were painfully candid. Couples warned us not to gloss over realities, for losing the health and energies of youth is no small thing.

Agreed! We're personally far from naïve about the challenges of the later years. After all, we're both well into the second half ourselves. Both our wives have experienced serious medical issues. Yet, it's also when many good things can happen: the ability to cherish the small things, deep, strong knowledge of your mate (and yourself), a relieved sense of *not* having to keep up with the Joneses.

But for a growing number of couples in the second half, all of this is not enough. Boomer divorces are rising. Still others feel trapped and decidedly unhappy. Length alone is not enough. What's happening? Why are there such contrasts between couples that are miserable, or stoically resigned in their marriages, and those who, as one friend of ours said, are happily "joined at the hip"?

Obviously, answers are legion. Mates come into marriages with issues; unhappy marriages can grind on year after year, deepening the ruts of pain and anger; sometimes illnesses and other severe events are just too much to handle. The *Is this all there is?* question hovers in the background.

At the same time, many of those who shared their stories came from difficult backgrounds. By this point in life, few, if any, have escaped the things life throws at us. So what makes the difference between the marriages that flourish and those that flounder? Three "traits of a long-term marriage" kept surfacing:

Laughter and acceptance. The couples who thrive see each other's imperfections and even their maddening habits, and after so many years they can at last laugh about them together. They accept themselves and each other for what they are, warts and all. One wife said, "I don't have to fix everything that's wrong with him and make him perfect. He still thinks he's helping me by taking his dirty plate and putting it next to the sink."

Resilience. As hard stories of reversals and grief flowed, we sensed the resilience in these men and women. The foundation for that resilience was their commitment to marriage. They viewed marriage as a covenant that enables us to stand with our spouse through the natural ups and downs and ebbs and flows of life.

Faith. The anchor for their commitment was their faith. They consistently told us it was core to their navigating personality clashes, wounds, and crises. Faith made possible moments of joy.

We are grateful for all the men and women who shared with us. (Some names and identifying details have been changed.) We also hear from marital veterans Jerry and Dianna Jenkins, Joni and Ken Tada, and John and Cindy Trent. All have written eloquently and honestly about marriage, but more important, all have "walked the talk." All were gracious enough to share their wisdom with us. We deeply appreciate their contributions.

And because couples of all ages need practical ideas, I (Gary) offer some pointers that we hope will enhance your relationship as a couple.

The book of Ecclesiastes tells us there's "a time for every purpose under heaven, a time to gain, and a time to lose . . . and that God has made everything beautiful in its season."

The beautiful season is a gift and a challenge. May we enter into it with zest and anticipation together.

—Gary Chapman and Harold Myra

PART ONE

1

Adventure: Saying Yes to Life

A young woman darts into a Paris café and catches a man's eye . . . a rich girl and poor guy fight off villains . . . lovers flee through the jungle to a cliff's edge. In the movies, romance means adventure: the thrill of danger, discovery, chase, and new love. Everything is exciting, exhilarating, and alluring! But Hollywood rarely associates adventure with marriage. Neither do we. If anything, we see it as quite the opposite. We say, "Why doesn't she get married and settle down?" Hollywood really doesn't associate adventure with the mature among us, with the notable exception of Dame Judi Dench finding love in India in the *Best Exotic Marigold* films.

But adventure *matters.* Adventure matters because for many of us, the temptation is to settle down and stay there. The "Marigold" movies resonated because they touched on questions so many of us ask, like: Who am I? Who are we? And what are we going to do in the time God gives us? What is the *more* that we may be missing?

We smiled at a friend's description of a recent moment in her marriage:

The older we get, the less patience we have with the Northern winter. One way we break up the bleakness is by visiting friends of ours with a home on an island off the Florida coast. Manatees, pelicans, palm trees, and the elemental feeling of warm salt water lapping your toes are truly balm to the frozen soul.

Best of all is the joy of hanging out with dear friends, just as we are, totally relaxed.

One evening, after a great meal, we were all chilling in front of the TV watching basketball. Everyone, including the two Labs, was in some stage of reclining. Ah, this is the life!

The next thing I knew, I was blinking and shaking off the fog of sleep. I'd nodded off and so had everyone else. Some late-night talk show was droning on. One husband was asleep on the couch. Another husband, asleep sitting up. A wife, curled up and snoozing. And both dogs were sprawled and snoring.

I loved the peculiar vulnerability of it all! When do our friends see us asleep? I was glad my husband and I weren't the only ones who "conk out" in front of the tube, mouths agape. It was all so comfy and cozy . . .

"FRESH TURNS AND NEW SURPRISES"

Comfy and cozy is great, but when are we *too* comfortable? When do we need to get off the recliner and make some changes?

Swiss psychiatrist Paul Tournier, in *The Adventure of Living,* writes that we never find fulfillment except by living in a spirit of adventure. He specifically applies that to all seasons of marriage: "To make a success of one's marriage, one must treat it as an adventure, with all the riches and difficulties that are involved in an adventure shared with another person."

Depending on your personality, "adventure" means many things. For some who are wed to their routines, it could mean taking a different route to the grocery store. But there are great riches for long-married partners in having something *new* to bring to the marriage: new ideas, new conversations, and new people to know. Newness and change, however modest, wakes up the brain, even carving new neural paths. It's good for our marriages and good for our health.

But newness is not necessarily the same thing as novelty. Many of us have known couples whose later years seemed to consist of an empty pursuit of pleasure. Yet neither do we want to remain stuck in our comfortable rut. Listen to psychiatrist Tournier, who writes that all through life we need fresh adventures and that we find shared purposes in them by "waiting on God for a new beginning."

Here is his marriage prescription: "The surrendered life is an adventure because it is always on the alert, listening to God, to His voice and to His angels! It is an absorbing puzzle, an exciting search for signs of God." Tournier describes the adventure of faith as "exciting, difficult, and exacting, but full of poetry, of new discoveries, of fresh turns and new surprises. Saying 'Yes' to God is saying 'Yes' to life. Marriage can be turned into an adventure again, even when it has become a mere institution, a habit, or even a bore."[1]

LESS SPACE, MORE MARGIN

Many empty-nesters wonder about selling the big suburban house and moving to a quaint country cottage or sleek city apartment in a walkable neighborhood. We read those endless "Top Places to Retire" lists online and wonder how we would fare in, say, the Carolinas. But Paul and Becky actually did more than think about it.

The couple recently moved from the farthest reaches of exurbia to a city condo with an incredible water view, trading Paul's grinding two-hour commute for a twelve-minute jaunt on the bus to his downtown job. In the morning the sunrise floods their bedroom and sparkles off the water (although, Paul says, without shades "it's like 125 degrees in here when the sun comes in"). They walk everywhere, actually talk to their new urban neighbors, have found a church with many young people, and in general feel much more relaxed.

> **"I thought, 'if we're this separated at fifty, what will it look like when we're seventy?'"**

For Becky and Paul, the move to the city is actually a homecoming of sorts. They began their married life in the city and vowed that eventually they would return to the city.

But first they wanted to raise their large family in the suburbs. "It was Paul laying down his life for his family," Becky said. "When I would come into the city, I would wonder, 'How is he able to do this?'"

"I was always exhausted," Paul said. "You become obsessed with sleep. I kept asking, 'If I go to bed at such-and-such a time, how many hours will I get?' Becky and I were living very separate lives. I thought, 'If we're this separated at fifty, what will it look like when we're seventy?'"

When the kids were grown and Paul was promoted, it seemed the right time to move. Then, their eldest daughter came home for a visit, looked at her father, and said, "if this keeps up, you are going to be dead. I want my kids to have grandparents." And she "ordered" them to move to the city.

Now it was time for Becky to sacrifice. "It was very difficult for her to shut down her life so we could have a joint life," Paul said. "But for us to have that joint life, it was necessary."

"And part of this new season is that we're each more in touch with what the other is going through," Becky says.

"WE WERE WORKING TOGETHER AT SOMETHING"

Kevin and Karen are adventurers too. They don't fit the typical image. Both serve on the staff at a local church. They don't take exotic vacations (unless you count a trip Kevin took to visit a "sister" church in Nigeria a few years back). They've lived in the same house for a long time. But Kevin and Karen have found adventure and renewal in pursuing a "shared purpose."

Kevin and Karen made a marriage-changing discovery when their two children were small. They had been leading a church youth group in which the kids were so rude they wanted to quit. It strained their relationship, yet the discouragement also forced them to talk more to each other.

Here is what they discovered:

"The biggest surprise was that something good was happening

to our marriage. We were working together at something. What a puzzle! That youth-group ministry, which by all rights should have pulled our marriage apart, actually bonded it in a new level of intimacy."

Their "working together at something" became more than a shared task. They wrote a book titled *More than You and Me*, which summed up their vision of marriage as a means to serving others.

Since leading that youth group decades ago, Kevin and Karen have experienced heavy personal challenges: difficulties with kids, hard times in the life of the church, even chronic physical pain, but they still reach out as a team to help others. Recently they asked four younger couples to meet at their house to talk about life issues. "These are couples heavily involved in the church and wanting to grow. Helping other couples is a thing we love to do together."

Now Kevin has taken a new job, returning to the publishing world he joined thirty years ago. But, always the pastor, he will continue to be involved at the church where he and Karen serve. And amid all their busyness, it's safe to say that they will continue making their marriage something that serves others, and having adventures along the way.

"WHEN WE LOST MOST OF OUR RETIREMENT, THE CHOICE WAS OURS"

Making marriage an adventure rather than a bore takes two people, and sometimes those two people are very different. What about individual talents, preferences, and drives? How does a couple embrace a shared purpose when they are male and female, "Mars and Venus," unique individuals?

We found Ted and Linda's experiences relevant to those questions. Right now they're living a fairly unique adventure. They decided to live on a boat. No, not a big houseboat but a very small boat with only 350 square feet of living space. How did they end up on a boat? A few years ago the Great Recession wiped out the equity in their home. The next year the Securities & Exchange Commission (SEC) called, informing them two men they trusted were actually running a Ponzi scheme, defrauding them out of their life savings. The men ended up in prison, and Ted and Linda ended up no longer able to afford a house or rent payments.

They had few options.

"We'd always sort of wanted to live on the water," Ted says, "so it wasn't much of a stretch to turn the financial downturn into the opportunity to create an adventure. We set our sights on a boat."

It became a long adventure on a small boat! In those tight quarters month after month, how do two very different people cope? Early in their marriage they each crafted a personal mission statement, and they also crafted one as a couple. Now this intrigued us. They implemented their personal statements, yet mostly ignored the combined one.

Why did the mutual mission statement gather dust? Here's what they told us: "The individual statements of purpose were what helped us blend as a couple." That may seem contradictory, but it says this, that mutual respect for what the other brings to a marriage is essential.

Yet after decades of marriage, new dynamics created new

tensions, such as absorbing the emotional impact of their financial losses.

"When we lost most of our retirement, the choice was ours," Ted says. "We could become woeful in our loss, or we could see what life could be like in a completely different environment. Trusting God for provision is a real thing for us. So is our gratitude for it. Many times we ask, 'What's next? How will He provide? Will we move into a real house where the grandkids can visit more often?' We come back to this: we get to live on a boat, fulfilling a dream, learning to trust our Master for next steps."

UNDERSTANDING "THE OTHER"

A touch of wildness, a sense of purpose and adventure, and a commitment to shared goals, these energize and deepen a marriage. It means empowering a mate's gifts and growth year after year. It means not slipping from comfort into stagnation. Often it means sacrifice.

The other. The only way for marriage to flourish at whatever age is for the "other," that most important person in our lives, to be understood, included, and listened to. If a marriage is to last, the partners must be on the same page, especially at major crossroads. Mates may share values but sharply disagree about which path they should take.

Like other couples, long ago Jeanette and I (Harold) made choices that now define our lives. On three very big choices, it was Jeanette who insisted we make those choices in full agreement.

At her initiative we had become foster parents, and eventually a little boy named Ricky needed to be adopted. However, our plates were more than full with our three older birth children and heavy pressures at my work. We were far past the usual age to adopt.

We prayed and repeatedly discussed this huge fork in the road. Jeanette was adamant in saying, "No way should we do this if you aren't fully making this decision with me."

Three times we were confronted with the clear need to adopt a child. Three times we mutually, after much prayer and discussion, said yes.

Tough times always come, and to us they came in severe measure. Jeanette's insistence that we be of one mind on the adoptions was proven right. How easily the blame game can start! "If only *you* hadn't . . ."

In action movies, when partners lack agreement and one wanders off, it usually spells disaster. In contrast, determination to find common ground, or to fully affirm a mutual choice, makes relevant this scriptural wisdom, "Two are better than one . . . if one falls down, his friend can help him up" (Ecclesiastes 4:9).

SPENDING YOUR "BONUS YEARS"

Demographers tell us there's a new thing under the sun: twenty or thirty or more "bonus years" of life expectancy. Psychologist Erik Erikson termed this a time of "generativity," when seasoned adults can pass on wisdom and values to the next generations.

The extended time of "generativity" is being well used by many couples who see it as a gift. Joe and Marilyn, whose house is a thoroughfare for grandchildren and international visitors, travel often to Brazil to help their daughter and her family in the ministry to street children in Sao Paulo.

Their natural instinct for adventure started early. Joe, a high diver, first noticed Marilyn when she broke from a group of girls as the only one to brave the high dive at a pool. That began a marriage without borders. With their small children they drove and camped for six weeks from Scotland to Beirut, where Joe began teaching. Three years later, when settled back home in the Midwest, an unexpected opportunity came to teach in Nigeria. Although their children balked at moving again so soon, Marilyn asked, "Why not go?" They did.

We asked how they worked out their differences, and they could remember only one heated argument. Joe was teaching at the American University in Cairo and would eat lunch with a mostly Muslim group. Out of courtesy, he decided to fast with them during Ramadan, and Marilyn strongly disagreed. She admitted to being mad at him.

"How long were you mad?" we asked.

"All through the month of Ramadan!"

But despite the challenges of crossing borders and cultures, Marilyn and Joe would have it no other way. "Without adventure, life would be boring," Marilyn says. "It puts spark in your life."

"GOD HAS MUCH MORE FOR US"

Yet not every couple is ready, or able, to fly to Brazil or move to an urban high-rise. Shared purpose and a spirit of adventure will look different for everyone, depending on personalities and the realities of health and finances.

One couple agreed to take care of their married daughter's pets for a season: the dog, fish, and birds. They acknowledged that the experience enlivened their home. "It broke our routines and forced us to care for other creatures. You can get really ingrown as empty nesters, with your tidy house and careful little routines. Neither of us is wired to be big risk-takers, and we've come to terms with that, but we're always thinking about where *is* the adventure for us. I like coming home to the squawking of the parakeets and the dog's chew toys left strewn all over and the fish wriggling to tell me he's hungry. I think it's good for us."

This same couple recently moved to an Anglican congregation. They say the adventure of a younger, larger, more liturgical setting has been a needed change. "The worship is very joyful, very creative, and yet ancient and solemn at the same time. We like the Bible-based, strongly relevant preaching. We can each see how the other has grown spiritually. We used to bicker on the way to church. Now we go to bed on Saturday nights excited about worship the next day. We talk about how we can contribute. It feels new and energizing. We believe God has much more for us."

Each of us is responsible for living with a spirit of adventure.

PLUNGING IN

One husband said, "I look back on years of fast-track everything: work pressures, kids in school and tons of activities, always being stretched, and wondering what was coming next. Yes, it was an adventure, and everything is different now. Yet in a sense, it's the same, always a new day with choices to make and people to love. That will even be true if my health fails and I'm flat on my back."

Jerry and Shirley Rose in their book *Significant Living* challenge us as we age "not to back off from new adventures when God is just as dependable as ever." To illustrate, they use their white-water rafting experience. "The river," they write, "was an adventure with rough spots and awesome, truly majestic scenery." They had to submit themselves to the will of the river, knowing they wouldn't get lost, and would experience adventures along the way. Referring specifically to the second half of life, they conclude, "We can experience more thrills, bear more fruit, and live significantly by plunging in and getting in God's flow."[2]

HOW TO BUILD AN ADVENTUROUS MARRIAGE

Adventure doesn't mean you have to do something as drastic as living on a boat. Adventure may be trying a different restaurant, or going to a high school football game to watch the grandson of a friend. Then on Monday send him a note and tell him how much you enjoyed watching him play. Adventure can also be a ministry.

Not all adventure is a shared experience. Each of us is responsible for living with a spirit of adventure. I (Gary) am a morning person. I enjoy spending an hour in the wooded area behind our house cutting kudzu vines (if you don't live in the Southeast, you will not know what kudzu is). It is a large, leafy, fast-growing vine that climbs trees, and ultimately kills the tree. So, I guess you'd say I'm a tree hugger. When I cut the vine at the ground level, it dies and eventually falls from the trees. I love the adventure I experience while working in the woods. My wife, Karolyn, is a night person. She will never venture into the woods with me in the early morning hours, even if she were a morning person. She's far too concerned about snakes, ticks, and poison ivy. Yet she enjoys hearing about my adventures when I share with her the sights and sounds I experienced in the woods.

On the other hand, Karolyn is a symphony lover. I really wish that I could hear the sounds and distinguish the instruments as she does, but I am not a musician, and my mind is not wired to hear all the distinguishing sounds. To her, attending the symphony is an adventure. When she returns from attending the symphony with some of her close friends, I enjoy hearing her tell me about what she experienced. My joy is in seeing the spirit of adventure still alive in her heart and eyes as she shares with me.

Giving each other the freedom to develop the spirit of adventure in different venues is one of the keys to having an adventurous marriage.

SUGGESTIONS FOR STIMULATING ADVENTURE IN YOUR MARRIAGE

1. Take a ceramics class together.
2. Encourage your creative spouse to take art lessons.
3. Visit each other's hometown. Show them where you were born, went to school, church, etc. Make the trip even livelier by taking the grandchildren.
4. Volunteer to work together at the local soup kitchen.
5. Revisit your honeymoon destination.
6. Volunteer for a mission trip, at home or abroad.

7. Once a year visit a different church in your city.
8. Take a train ride to somewhere.
9. Go to your high school or college reunion.
10. In June, go shopping for Christmas presents.

We encourage you to make your own list of things you would like to do, as individuals or as a couple.

2

Meeting in the Middle: The Dance of Differences

Before Brad was married he dreamed about how wonderful it would be to get up every morning and have breakfast with his wife, Jennifer. After he was married he found out that Jennifer did not do mornings. He dreamed of hiking and overnight camping, but he discovered that the Hilton Garden Inn was her idea of overnight camping. He believed in saving money. In fact, he paid cash for the ring (it was a discreetly small one). Her philosophy was, "Shop today; you may be sick tomorrow." Brad believed there was a rational answer for everything. "Now let's think about this" was his favorite statement. "I'm tired of thinking. Why can't we just for once do what we want to do without thinking about it?" was Jennifer's response.

Chances are, as you look back on your own early years together, you discovered some of these same differences. One of the most important lessons we can learn in marriage is this truth: Your spouse is not like you. Even if the two of you are extremely similar, you are also extremely different.

"My husband and I grew up in the same town, just a couple of miles apart. We went to the same high school. We went to the same church. It was a big church so we didn't know each other. We're ethnically not that different, both fairly easygoing, and have more or less similar tastes in a lot of things. We've always been very compatible. An older professor we knew in our early years said we were 'hand in glove.'

"But over the years, I came to realize how different we are in some critical ways that were not obvious. For example, I'm more intuitive, dreaming about the future. He is more immediate and in the moment. Understanding that has been huge in our thirty-some years of marriage, but it took awhile."

Whether you agree with the Mars/Venus analogy that men and women are from different planets, or if you think those ideas are overblown, a host of variables ensures differences in every marriage.

In addition to male/female dynamics, even two introverts or two extroverts raised in similar homes face differences developed from: growing up with siblings or lack of them, parental styles, school and job experiences, temperament, and love languages. The list is endless.

All those differences can be celebrated, or at least accepted, or they can rub like sand in a shoe.

In my book *The Marriage You've Always Wanted,* I (Gary) wrote about Jason, who told me about his marriage that ended in divorce. He now realizes he destroyed his own marriage. "I allowed my emotions to control my life. Because we were so different, Susan did a lot of things that irritated me. It seemed that almost every day I was telling her that I was hurt, disappointed, frustrated, and angry. It all came across as condemnation to her. I was trying to be open, but I realize now you can't let raw sewage run through a marriage and expect to grow a garden."

Jason's right. It may not be easy to adjust to differences and to dance with someone who spins when you dip, but it's possible. The couples we talked to learned to flex and communicate mutual esteem and love. One couple with major personality differences told us this:

"When we were first married, we liked the quote, 'It's not finding the right person but *being* the right person.' However, in the early years, we didn't realize how different we were. We kept learning about each other. We eventually discovered that instead of trying to get the other person to change, it was better to move toward the middle."

"SHE KNOWS I CAN'T HELP WHO I AM"

Another couple said, "It's accepting the other person as is." A husband gave us this example:

"My wife comes alive at social functions. She's not big on games, but when people play Charades and start laughing and yelling, she's in her element.

"I endure social gatherings. I'm a one-on-one person, and games like Charades make me feel foolish. I'm fairly smart, but I don't think fast.

"We were at a party recently and everyone had to participate. I tried to get into the spirit and laugh with everyone else, but it all just felt silly. When it was my turn, I took a pass.

"Here's my point: Although my wife nudged me once with

a whisper, 'Lighten up,' she did it with a touch of humor and never once mentioned it on the way home or after. Years ago we would have had a dispiriting discussion about how I can spoil a good evening, but she knows I can't help who I am. I've learned to enjoy the fact that she's having a good time even if I'm not." A willingness to respect the personality and interests of your spouse may be the first step toward harmony.

LEARNING THE 5 LOVE LANGUAGES

However, time alone does not heal all differences. That is why my (Gary's) counseling office has seen a steady stream of couples over the years. Some of the differences, as with Jason and his wife, are deep and hurtful. Other differences may not be as profound, but they can bring very real pain to a marriage. I have found that understanding each other's primary love language, and choosing to speak it on a regular basis, creates a positive emotional climate in which we can assess our differences, and learn how to make them assets, rather than liabilities.

Let me briefly summarize the five love languages.

1. *Words of Affirmation*—using words to affirm your spouse. "You look nice in that outfit." "I really appreciate what you did for me." "One thing I really like about you is . . ."
2. *Acts of Service*—doing things for your spouse that you know they would like for you to do: help cooking meals, washing dishes, vacuum floors, mowing the grass, washing the car, cleaning the garage, and so

forth. If this is the love language of your spouse, then "actions speak louder than words."

3. *Gifts*—it is universal to give gifts as an expression of love. A gift says, "He was thinking about me," or "Look what she got for me."
4. *Quality Time*—giving your spouse your undivided attention. I am not talking about sitting on the couch watching television. Someone else has your attention. I'm talking about sitting together with the TV off, looking at each other, talking and listening. Or, taking a walk together as you talk.
5. *Physical Touch*—holding hands, embracing, kissing, the whole sexual part of marriage, arm on their shoulder as you pour a cup of coffee, driving down the road and putting your hand on your spouse's neck.

The basic concept is that out of these five languages, each of us has a primary love language. One speaks more deeply to us emotionally than the other four. It is very similar to spoken language. Each of us grew up speaking a language with a dialect. That's the one we understand best. The same thing is true in speaking love. If you speak your own love language and not your spouse's love language, it will not mean to them what it would mean to you. Many couples have missed each other emotionally for years because they have not learned to speak their spouse's primary love language.

If this concept is new to you, you may want to go online and take the free profile to help you determine each of your primary love languages. Visit www.5lovelanguages.com. When you speak each other's love language on a regular basis, you create a positive climate in which the two of you can process differences much more easily.

"AT TIMES I JUST WANTED TO QUIT LIFE"

Counselors, for good reasons, probe for facts about a client's "family of origin." Our growing-up experiences profoundly affect us. They certainly shaped John and Sharon.

Sharon describes herself as coming into their marriage stable, very protected, and naïve. "I lived at home till I was married. I was twenty-five going on fourteen! I didn't know that when you have a new baby you don't sleep. I had a Pollyanna view of life; nothing bad could happen."

In contrast John says, "I grew up living on a narrow ledge on a windy precipice. I had no stability, no security. If anything good happened for me, then something bad was coming."

"People used to tell us it gets better in your fifties. Really?"

Over the years, raising three sons, they made many adjustments. For instance, at a Bible study Sharon would come looking for "nourishment," while John would be asking, "Why, why, why?" John's way of handling stress was to go for long runs, and when first married, they agreed he would be her trainer. That lasted a very short time.

It was when their sons were leaving the nest and getting married, they faced their biggest adjustments. After decades of steady employment, John lost his job.

"People used to tell us it gets better in your fifties, that those are the great years," John says. "Really? What happened is not what we expected."

Sharon was stunned by their new vulnerability. "When something unfair happens, where do you go if you can't hold on? At times I wanted to just quit life. It was very hard. People who haven't had something awful happen to them don't realize that no one escapes. For me, growing up protected, it was a shock. But nothing shocked John."

Sharon was angry, but John was mostly disappointed in himself, believing, "A man has to provide." Tensions grew. "It was hard for John to deal with me." Differences were a big part of the problem.

He says, "I like the give-and-take." She responds, "I don't!"

John sees Sharon as strong and passionate, whereas she views him as the voice of reason. She "balances him out" and he "keeps her feet on the ground."

Sharon says during the past six years of troubles, she's been more aware of God in her life because she's had to look to Him and change her thinking. Years ago, she read an article in *Marriage Partnership* magazine about long marriages and the reason couples stayed together. "I still remember the conclusion. The couples said, 'It's because we didn't give up.'"

Sharon added, "I have finally learned, after going through these years, this fact of life: No matter how bad or good a situation is, *it will change.*"

POSTER CHILDREN FOR "OPPOSITES ATTRACT"

Every now and then you run into a couple who are true opposites. So it is with Andy and Phyllis. She's tall, energetic, always smiling, and decidedly a redhead. Andy looks like a serious professor, with graying beard and, on occasion, a twinkle in his eyes. Together they lead seminars for college students, and they have fun unpacking their differences.

Andy, with his bemused look, starts off with a short monologue:

Phyllis and I are the poster children for opposites attract.
She's an extrovert. I'm an introvert.

Phyllis cares passionately about the world.
I think about the world.

Phyllis thinks everyone she meets is fascinating and interesting.
I think the dictionary is fascinating and interesting.

Phyllis is a wonderful conversationalist who can make a fence post talk.
I am the fence post.

That last line cracks up the crowd, for they've experienced Phyllis's dynamism and warmth. And when the students hear they've been married for nearly forty years, they're stunned, and invariably the girls give a big round of applause. The young women are acutely aware of marriages that failed, and have very personal hopes that people can still stay married and actually enjoy it.

Andy and Phyllis tell the students it's okay to be attracted to someone with a different personality. What's crucial is having common values.

Still, differences can create marriage-busting problems and require "special handling." Andy estimates it took about twenty years to effectively negotiate disagreements. "When it gets hot between us, Phyllis wants to settle it immediately. But I need space and time to calm down. I don't want to react out of anger."

How did they adjust? "Two things happened," Andy says. "She realized that I would eventually come back, and we would fix it; and I learned over time to come back more quickly."

Phyllis adds, "I learned he really was afraid of what he might say."

"We've had our 'knock-down, drag-out arguments,'" says Andy, "but we've never insulted each other."

Working through differences is essential, but so is finding and affirming commonalities. For instance, although Andy and Phyllis are opposites in many ways, they're both "list people" who work toward getting things done.

We asked if their four children make comments about their differences and Andy immediately said, "My nickname is Eeyore. I'm always called that."

The contrast seems fitting: lively Phyllis contrasted with gloomy Eeyore. Yet Andy's ready smile and droll wit make him far more complex than the Winnie-the-Pooh character. His daughter once said, "Dad is the most measured man I've ever met. He never does anything without thinking about it."

We are God-made originals. He made us unique so we could complement each other.

That characteristic helps a mate avoid troubles, but it can also lead to conflicts with a spontaneous spouse. For that reason they set out to form a family culture that included candor. Phyllis is the rare good sport who actually likes to be teased. She smiled when Andy told us about finding an odd but "perfect" definition of her name: "Phyllis, happy, but not coordinated." "I'm a klutz!" she admits.

The lesson here? Whether a couple is true opposites, like Andy and Phyllis, or just different, like Sharon and John, differences can either wear away at a marriage, or help that marriage to grow. A little laughter, some work at understanding how the "other" wants to be loved, and a lot of acceptance go a long way.

UNITY, NOT UNIFORMITY

While differences can be deadly, they can also be delightful. I (Gary) mentioned earlier that my wife is not a morning person. However, recently I discovered my wife in the kitchen at 7 a.m. This had not happened since the last child had left for college. First, I hit my head on the cabinet door that she had left open, and then rammed my elbow into the microwave door that she had left open. I turned to get a knife to cut my grapefruit, and in doing so, I almost tackled her. I apologized and then said, with all sincerity, "You know, darling, I am really glad that you are not a morning person."

I suddenly realized how my attitude had changed from the early days when I resented that she didn't bounce out of bed like

I did every morning. I realized how much I had come to enjoy eating breakfast with God (He is always awake). I enjoy the predictability that the only cabinet doors that will be open are the ones I open, and the only drawers that will be open are the ones I open. I had not only come to accept our differences; I was actually delighted in the differences.

Differences are rooted in the fact that we are creatures of God. God is infinitely creative. No two of His creatures are exactly alike. We are God-made originals. The Scriptures say that in marriage the two become one. But that oneness does not mean uniformity; rather it means unity. God did not intend for us to be alike. Differences are there so we can complement each other, and strengthen our effectiveness in serving Christ.

Unfortunately, in the real world of marriage, differences have often driven couples to near delirium. Surely this is not God's intention. Differences are part of God's plan. The key is to make our differences an asset rather than a liability, to make our differences work for us rather than against us.

We suggest that you make a list of those differences you have discovered in each other through the years. Then ask these questions.

1. Which of these differences is still divisive in our relationship?
2. Which of these differences have we come to accept in each other?
3. Which of these have we truly come to see as an asset?
4. What steps can we take to make our differences delightful?

Use the following list of personality differences to help you construct your own list of differences.[3]

1. Dead Sea Stores thoughts and feelings. Talks little.	**Babbling Brook** Tells all. Whatever they hear, see, or think, they tell.
2. Robin Rises early, alert and singing. "The early bird gets the worm."	**Owl** Awake at night but come morning, the "do not disturb" sign is on the door.
3. Aggressive "Let's go get it." "Let's make it happen." "Seize the day."	**Passive** "Let's wait till it comes to us." "Everything comes to him who waits."
4. Neatnik "A place for everything and everything in its place" is their theme.	**Slob** "Where is it?" is their most asked question.
5. Planner Plans ahead. Takes care of every detail.	**Spontaneous Doer** "Don't waste time planning. We'll work out the details as we go."
6. The Butterfly Flits from event to event. Life's a party.	**The Raccoon** "Can't we stay home tonight? I'm tired."
7. The Professor "Let's be logical." "Think about it."	**The Dancer** "I don't know why, I just do." "Why do I have to have a reason?"

8. First Class "It only costs $5 more to go first class. We deserve it."	**Economy** "We can save lots of money and economy is nice enough."
9. Reader "Why would anyone waste time watching TV when there are so many good books to read?"	**TV Addict** "It's my way of relaxing." "I don't like to read." "Besides, I don't watch that much TV."
10. Symphony Lover "Bravo, bravo!" "Don't you just love that Opus #12 in A minor?"	**Bluegrass Devotee** "Now that's real music; it tells a story." "Listen to that banjo."
11. The Jogger The aerobic exercise—jogging. "My goal is the marathon. Rain or shine, I'll be there."	**The Walker** "I don't want to ruin my knees by jogging. I want to enjoy the scenery as I walk."
12. Channel Surfer "Why waste time on commercials. I can watch three shows at once if I omit the commercials."	**Commercial Watcher** "Can't we just enjoy one program instead of seeing parts of three? Besides, we can talk during the commercial."

3

Children in Crisis

One of the couples we talked with told us the following joke:

> *One day a lawyer was surprised to be visited by a couple in their nineties. He asked why they had come.*
>
> *"We came to get a divorce."*
>
> *Perplexed, the lawyer scratched his head. "But why would you want to get a divorce at your age?" he asked. "Why now?"*
>
> *The couple looked at each other, smiled and then replied, "Oh, we've just been waiting till our children died."*

We laughed when we heard that. Why did it strike us as funny? Maybe because it's true! No matter how old they are, or how old we are, we never stop feeling responsible for our adult children. We never stop hurting with them and for them.

Certainly it isn't all crisis and turbulence with our grown children. For many of us our relationships with our grown children are deeply satisfying. We are past the hard days of adolescent strife. Most of us don't have to worry about filling out FAFSAs. There's nothing like the joy of seeing our kids thriving in careers, happy with the right partner, growing in the Lord, doing well in the world, and maybe living next door, like the family in *My Big Fat Greek Wedding*.

But it doesn't always turn out that way.

One wife said her greatest source of anxiety is her grown children, and she told us how her daughter would call her when having a fight with her husband. "She tells me all the things he said that hurt her, and I get upset too. It's hard to sleep. But then the next time I see them, they've made up and they're fine!"

Mothers never stop worrying. Joy, the mom of four grown children, said, "I want to see them happy." She worries the most about her thirtysomething son's misery in his current job and his inability to find his niche in life. "He's really paralyzed," she said. She also worries about her thirty-two-year-old unmarried daughter. "I think about that biological clock . . ."

"WE DIDN'T KNOW IF WE WERE GOING TO MAKE IT THROUGH"

David and Pamela were experiencing good times in their marriage, long past the struggles of adapting to different parenting styles and their three major moves. But an unexpected diagnosis roiled their smoother waters. One of their married sons, who had a daughter, learned he was going blind. He was an athlete and a long-distance cyclist, and he was devastated by the prospect. The news felt impossible to accept.

David describes that time as "a deep, grieving season. I didn't feel I could do anything. I felt inept, yet I wanted to do something. I felt helpless, impotent, and it made me angry."

Pamela said, "Even though I was eating, I was losing a lot of weight. Seeing David so down made me feel things were never going to be the same. I couldn't talk about it."

"We just felt beaten up," David said. "For a year or two Pamela and I took it very hard. We didn't know if we were going to make it through."

There's nothing like the joy of seeing our kids thriving . . . but it doesn't always turn out that way.

"What helped?" we asked.

"Time," Pamela said. "You just have to hold on."

David remembered a turning point when his son became courageous in dealing with the loss of his sight. "His courage led us to accept the new normal."

He paused. "At the same time, you have moments when you say, 'This really stinks. Our son can't see his daughter.'"

Their son is still grappling with his blindness. Despite his disability, he recently completed a hundred-mile bike trip with a partner and continues to take on as many responsibilities as he can.

The crisis has further deepened David and Pamela's relationship. Recently their daughter observed, "You two are better together now than you ever were."

"It feels that way," Pamela said. "During most of our marriage, David was under pressure at work. There were times when I thought, 'I could do this easier on my own.' But now we're in a good place."

"Marriage is made for the long haul," David said. "It's a sacrament that shouldn't be taken lightly. There's joy in looking back. It's long-term for a reason."

"WE SAW THE SPLIT COMING FOR A LONG TIME"

Few crises rock a parent's world like their kids' marital struggles. We know the dismal statistics. Many of us have a sibling who divorced and remarried. But our kids, that's another story. One woman said, "When our daughter and her husband started having problems, one of the things that really grieved me was the idea that our modeling of a healthy marriage had failed. We saw peers of ours whose grown kids were following the script, marrying young, and having kids. That was hard."

We asked several couples who have watched their children divorce to share their experiences and insights. Here are a few:

> ****Some years ago both of us faced serious health issues, and we decided to move cross-country so we'd be near our daughter's family when we ended up in a nursing facility. We had no idea her husband was an alcoholic, and for a time, neither did she. But all those hunting trips involved alcohol, and, eventually, on his days off our grandchildren saw their dad drunk. Our daughter didn't ask our advice when she divorced him, but we understood she had little choice.*
>
> *For us, after five years of good medical care and helping each other stay very active, we're still able to help with the children and to attend their sports and school activities. We're very sad about the divorce, but we tell each other that*

if the marriage hadn't happened, we wouldn't have these grandkids we love so much. We feel sorry for their father who is missing all the wonderful things they're doing! We feel we're privileged to be rooting them on and providing support.

****We always had wonderful relationships with our son and daughter, and we love their marriage partners. We still do, and we understand the reasons for their divorces. But it's very hard. We never thought it would be this way. Yet we look at what we can be grateful for. Despite their troubles, all four parents are devoted to their kids, and they get along with each other. We spend lots of time with them all, loving them and helping out, investing ourselves in our children, their ex-spouses, and our grandchildren.*

****We saw the split coming for a long time. In some ways it's better that they're now functioning separately. We're determined to not let this be a dark cloud over us but to stay strong and healthy ourselves. If we do, we can be there as stable, loving grandparents for everyone involved. We continue to work at our marriage to keep it vital, not dwelling on all the negatives but embracing what's good about our lives right now.*

"YOU DON'T NEED TO PARENT ME ANYMORE"

Just when we may be facing major transitions ourselves, struggling with a health issue or job change or simply a loss of energy, here come our kids. One couple answered a call in the middle of the night from a son who had gotten into a fight with a roommate, with police involved and friends turning against him. It took them a long time to get back to sleep, and the next day was hard and frustrating, trying to be helpful at a distance and wondering if they were wise in their responses.

The culture we live in doesn't help. We've heard all the data about millennials drifting away from faith. Changes in sexual mores unsettle even those of us who came of age in the "free love" era. But the clashes between Greg and Lisa and their daughter Sarah were sharper than most.

Lisa and Greg were childhood sweethearts, growing up as missionary kids. "We grew up with boundaries, viewing them as there to protect us, not limit us. But Sarah viewed them as a punitive fence. In junior high she was bombarded on the Internet by American secularism. Her friends saw nothing wrong with phone calls at 1 a.m. or texting at 3 a.m. We had a saying, 'Nothing good happens after midnight.' Naturally there are exceptions, but we emphasized that if you're always pushing boundaries, you invite trouble."

Sarah saw it differently. At age fourteen she told them, "You've done a great job of parenting, but you don't need to parent me anymore. I don't need you monitoring my Internet use, telling me what I should not wear, having to know where I am all the time, or caring so much about the friends I choose."

Greg responded, "Well, Sarah, that's great. Where are you going to live?"

Her answer: "By law you have to care for me till I'm eighteen. I just don't need you to tell me what to do."

Greg and Lisa knew they needed counseling and found significant help. Sarah participated, from tenth grade through her first year in college. Referring to their counselor, Lisa says, "Carol saved the life of our family." Still, Sarah kept making her own choices, crossing boundaries, sometimes raising her parents' hopes, but more often dashing them.

Ironically, it was when their hopes were high after she'd broken off an unhealthy relationship and reaffirmed her faith that Sarah came to them in tears. She said she might be pregnant after an unfortunate night that included alcohol.

The day they received confirmation of her pregnancy, they wept together, prayed, and read a lot of Scripture, including Isaiah 30:18: "The Lord must wait for you to come to him so he can show you his love and compassion. For the Lord is a faithful God. Blessed are those who wait for his help." They found challenge and solace in Psalm 143:8: "Let me hear of your unfailing love each morning, for I am trusting you. Show me where to walk, for I give myself to you" (both NLT).

Lisa and Greg found themselves in a delicate dance. Sarah didn't want them to tell anyone. When she was three months along, they told her this was her story but also their story, and they wanted to share it with their closest friends. Sarah reluctantly agreed, and they continued the journey.

Greg told us, "You've never met two people more opposite than Lisa and me." With Lisa as "an extraordinary listener and compassionate voice of reason," and Greg as "rational but sometimes too direct," they spent many hours in discussion. "There was so much to sort out and understand. We gave each other freedom to grieve, weep, and contemplate. We prayed together, and with Sarah."

They realized early on that the decision to keep the baby or give it up for adoption had to be their daughter's. "She never asked our opinion, and we never gave it. If we had, she might be tempted to say five years later, 'That wasn't really my decision.' She had to own it."

They also wanted to be wise about how she could receive grace from their church family. What happened next was redemptive beyond their imagination.

Sarah met with two of their pastors. This led to a meeting between the family and friends from the church. After Sarah shared her situation, and after an appropriate silence, the first to speak was a professor from a nearby college. Mentioning his own failures, he said, "I'm as broken as you are." One after another, those who had come confessed their own brokenness and spoke of God's mercy, grace, and love. When they had finished sharing, they had Sarah sit on a chair and placed their hands on her and prayed for her. Greg wept. Lisa remembers the moment as "a wonderful gift. We experienced that our church is a safe place to be."

Sarah later stood before the full congregation and thanked them for their love and said she was working with an adoption agency. But, she added, "Even as God redeems this, how can I learn to live without regretting my actions and their consequences? I'm not sure it's possible. Seeking forgiveness of those I've hurt requires humility that I don't possess. Forgiving myself requires grace and mercy that is not mine to give." Yet in the months that followed Sarah learned to trust God and He used this experience to renew her relationship with Himself and with her parents, and bring joy to many.

Lisa told us how much Elisa Morgan's book *The Beauty of Broken* resonated with their experience. As she showed us a photo of her grandson, Lisa's smile said she saw in her grandson the beauty of God's faithfulness.

HOW DO YOU DEAL WITH THE PAIN?

Through the years I (Gary) have wept with a number of couples who have walked the road of Greg and Lisa—an unmarried daughter who is pregnant or an unmarried son who has gotten a girl pregnant. Sometimes it has been grandparents whose lovely granddaughter has come home from college pregnant, or a grandson admits that he has failed morally. How do we as parents and grandparents do the right thing when our children and grandchildren have done the wrong thing?

Let me suggest the following:

1. *Don't blame yourself.* The first thought that comes to the mind of many parents is "What did we do wrong?" It is the logical question, but we cannot take responsibility for the choices of our children and grandchildren. Parents cannot be in the physical presence of their teenagers or young adults twenty-four hours a day and control their behavior. Choices expand in the teenage years, and poor choices produce detrimental results.
2. *Don't preach to your son or daughter.* Usually they are already feeling guilty. They know when their behavior

hurts their parents. They are aware when they violate the moral codes they have been taught. "Why did you do this?" "How could you do this to us?" "Don't you know you are tearing our hearts apart?" "I can't believe you could be so stupid!" Such statements will only compound the problem, and will never bring healing to the soul of your child.

3. *Don't try to fix it.* The natural response of many parents is to try to minimize what has happened. They jump into a "damage control" mode and try to protect their son or daughter. In my opinion, this is an extremely unwise move. The young adult must learn to accept responsibility for the decisions they have made.
4. *Give your young adult unconditional love.* Allowing him or her to experience the consequences of their own failure is in itself an act of love. In so doing, you are looking out for the well-being of your daughter or son, which is the essence of love. If you know their love language, this is the time to speak their primary love language loudly, while giving the other four love languages as often as possible. Your child's moral failure creates feelings of guilt. These emotions push them away from you. As Adam and Eve tried to hide in the garden from the presence of God, so your son or daughter will try to hide from you.

Daniel and Mickey told me that when their son arrived home from college, having told them on the phone that he had gotten a girl pregnant, they met him at the door with outstretched arms. They each gave him a long, tearful embrace and said, "We love you." Then they sat down and listened as he confessed his wrongdoing and asked for their forgiveness.

5. *Listen with empathy*. Empathy means to enter into the feelings of another. Parents need to put themselves into the shoes of their young adult and try to understand what led to the failure, as well as what their son or daughter is feeling at the moment.
6. *Give them support*. Let your child know that while you are deeply hurt and cannot remove all the consequences, you want him/her to know that you are with them and will stand by their side as they walk through the consequences of dealing with this failure.
7. *Give guidance to your young adult or teenager.* By guidance, I do not mean manipulation. When the parents decide what ought to be done, and try to convince their child to do it, this is manipulation. Guidance is helping the teenager think through the situation and make wise choices in responding to the consequences of the moral failure. Other ways in which parents may give guidance to a young adult is by helping them follow their own thoughts to their logical conclusion by asking questions, rather than making statements. To be a responsible parent or grandparent is to help your teen or young adult learn from their mistakes. If you are walking the road of Greg and Lisa, we hope you will find these suggestions helpful.

LIVING WITH SUBSTANCE ABUSE: "THANK YOU FOR NOT GIVING UP ON ME"

There are other poor decisions on the part of children and grandchildren that bring deep pain to parents and grandparents. Those whose children wrestle with addiction bear a crushing burden. Having an addicted son or daughter can take over a couple's lives for years. They find themselves torn in a maelstrom, wreaking havoc on their family, their finances, and their hopes. Their child's betraying them time after time after time grinds into them the realization the addiction trumps any promises a child makes. From crisis to crisis, nothing they do changes the fact that their son or daughter lives on death's edge.

When you talk to such couples, it's soon evident this is the great drama of their lives. In ways similar to soldiers imprinted by war's anguish, they tell of being driven year after year toward the pit of despair.

Yet those we talked to not only held on to hope through it all, but, through prayer and love, AA and other resources, their children beat the sobering odds and finally made it into lives of drug abstinence.

The years of getting there were grim. Crises would repeatedly land a son or daughter in residential treatments, at great expense. Multiple diagnoses churned up confusion and disappointments. Suicide attempts would come close to succeeding. Hopes would endlessly rise but be dashed, and persistent prayers seemed to have no effect.

Yet these couples stayed steady in their love and resilience.

One son, now happily married and drug-free, recently said to his parents, "Thank you for not giving up on me."

How did these couples not give up? Here are some of the things we heard:

> ****These experiences can break up a marriage. No matter what's going on, you have to intentionally love and reach out to your spouse.*
>
> ****I took to heart a sermon I heard called "The King Has One More Move." The story is that in a museum a chess expert studied a painting titled* Checkmate. *He decided the painting had to be either retitled or repainted, because the king had one more move. The message to us was, "We're not checkmated. God has at least one more move for us and our family."*
>
> ****We read a book titled* Don't Let Your Kids Kill You. *It wasn't a great book, but it gave a little hope, and it connected us with other couples with addicted kids. We learned that detachment is a spiritual discipline.*
>
> ****During this time I decided that the second half of my life would not be about the kids but about my wife. I needed to invest in her.*
>
> ****I knew people were judging us. They'd say, "I don't understand, you seem like great parents." I just beat myself up*

until I shared all this with a pastor. He said to me, "Your son made choices. Think about this: Adam in the garden of Eden made choices too, and he had the perfect Father."

HOW DO WE SET BOUNDARIES WITH OUR KIDS?

As parents we love our children and want to help, but how much can we do? How much should we do? Wise parents recognize that physical, emotional, and financial resources always have limits. The most common problem of parenting an adult child is to overreact to a crisis in the child's life, to become too involved. Remember that our goal in raising children is that they will become independent. If you step in too soon and too often, you may short-circuit the process of your child's emerging maturity. Your role is to give love, acceptance, encouragement, and guidance when requested.

Parents whose adult children are going through crises must maintain the balance between self-preservation and self-sacrifice. We must maintain our own health and well-being while trying to help our children as needed. Your physical, emotional, and spiritual health must be nourished, and you must focus on keeping your own marriage strong.

When they do not seek available help, parents often lose themselves while trying to save their children.

Often parents will disagree on what and how much they should do for their adult children. My advice is, if you cannot resolve conflicts related to your adult children, reach out for help. A Christian counselor or pastor will likely be able to help you make a wise decision. When they do not seek available help, parents often lose themselves while trying to save their children. Many an older couple have ended up divorcing each other after having expended all their energy trying to help their adult children, and failing to nurture their own relationship.

ENJOY YOUR GROWN CHILDREN—AND CHERISH YOUR SPOUSE

We want to end this chapter on a positive note. The reality is there are thousands of parents in the second half of marriage who have a wonderful relationship with their adult children. Karolyn and I (Gary) often remind each other how blessed we are to have two adult children who are committed followers of Christ, happily married, and pursuing their vocations with passion. While none of our children or grandchildren live in the same state as we, we keep in touch with each other by phone and texting. When we are together, we enjoy our relationships immensely.

One of the great joys in life is seeing your children and grandchildren seeking to live their lives in service to others. The apostle John said, "I have no greater joy than to hear that my children walk in truth." Enjoy your grown children, and pray for them. Let them live their own lives while you cherish your spouse.[4]

Jerry and Dianna Jenkins

"I STILL FEEL THAT HOME IS WHEREVER SHE IS"

BESTSELLING AUTHOR *Jerry B. Jenkins has written often and eloquently of his wife, Dianna, to whom he has been married for forty-five years. His book* Hedges *has influenced a couple of generations with its principles on protecting a marriage from temptation. And many are familiar with Jerry's stories of coming home from work when his three sons were young, devoting all his time to them, and writing only after they were in bed. We asked Jerry to share some thoughts about what it takes to remain lifelong "lovers and friends."*

You've written, "Love is an act of the will. Love is as love does." How has that played out over the years with Dianna?

I'm an incurable romantic. Though my father was a man's man, an ex-Marine and a career police chief, he was also chivalrous, a gentleman, a servant, and referred to my mother as his lifetime valentine in hundreds of poems he wrote her in their more than sixty years together. He was never too manly to wash dishes, mop a floor, or change a diaper (I resent him for that convicting example to this day).

He was not much for lectures, but his quiet model taught me that talk—and even the written word—can be cheap. It was the doing of his love that proved it.

Dianna is the hardier, harder working, and healthier of the two of us. During our forty-five years of marriage, the only time she has been out of commission longer than half a day—believe it or not—was after having given birth three times and recuperating from back surgery twenty years ago. No cold or flu or any other ailment in all that time.

Many years ago I wrote a book entitled *12 Things I Want My Kids to Remember Forever,* and one of those things was "Women work harder than men." Had I ever doubted this, it was driven home to me during that surgery recoup season when I finally got the privilege of living out the wedding vow ". . . in sickness and in health."

For once I got to serve her! Under her tutelage as she lay mending, I even cooked an entire Thanksgiving

Day meal and was thrilled to hear her assure guests from her spot on the sofa in the other room that no, I had not simply purchased everything at the grocery store.

As we are now senior citizens and empty nesters—and she has been ridiculously healthy again since that aberration—love as an act of the will has taken the form of daily courtesies. How easily such can be neglected or forgotten in the routine of daily life, but I remind myself that the apostle Paul's admonition to let nothing be done "through selfish ambition or conceit, but in lowliness of mind let each esteem others better than himself" (Philippians 2:3 NKJV) applies at home as much as at church or anywhere else.

We work at maintaining pleasantries and manners and politeness, even saying please and thank you and asking if the other wants or needs anything any time we're up. It may sound minor, but if there's only one portion of a favorite food left, we offer it to the other first.

If something's amiss, we're so averse to cold shoulders or making the other ferret out the reason for silence that we compete to see who can be first to clear the air. That doesn't mean we agree on everything. That's phony and a fool's game. But by respecting each other and talking, we honor each other's opinions.

We're so used to being lovers *and* friends that we often don't realize how rare this is until someone mentions it. Sometimes it's amusing, as if it's a surprise. "You seem to really like each other." Or, "You get along so well." Or, "It's obvious you're happy together."

We see some couples who appear to only tolerate each other, and I can't imagine living that way.

Early in your marriage, you and Dianna named your home Three Sons Acres. You've written about mounting poster-sized photos of your boys on your den walls and telling them daily you loved them. What effect has your love for your sons had on your marriage?

An old adage says something like, "The best thing a father can do for his children is to love their mother." I have found this correlation to that also true. Little thrills and fulfills Dianna more—or makes me more heroic to her—than my lavishing love and attention on our sons, and now our grandchildren.

At times when your sons were growing up, you'd tell them, "I love you even when you're ornery." When someone in your family gets ornery, how do you and your wife respond?

Humor is our default position. Of course this has to be used with discretion, because if someone is ***really*** exercised about something, you have to allow them a beat or two before they see any hilarity in the situation.

Dianna was enthusiastically chastising one of our sons when he was a teenager (all three are at least in their thirties now), for having gone out for the evening without cleaning his room. She was really letting him have it, reminding him that if she'd known, he wouldn't have gone, and now he was going to have to clean it before going to bed, and next time . . . etc.

When she paused for a breath, he said, "But I'm still going to be allowed to live here, right?"

Of course that cracked her up.

The "I love you even when you're ornery" line still works, even with grandkids. Three of our eight grands are adopted, and they're not above trying the most hurtful line they can think of when they're grouchy—something along the lines of wanting to go back where they came from.

It's been fun and gratifying to see our kids respond immediately with the affirmation we know the little ones crave. Dad or Mom will say, "Well, you know that'll never happen, because God gave you to us forever, and I'm never giving you up."

You make it a practice to say very positive things about Dianna in print and in public, admitting you're "quick to brag" about her resilience and beauty. What triggered this?

Frankly I'm not sure it's anything more than the Golden Rule. I've always enjoyed being funny, so I get pleasure from comedians. But it always bothers me when comics use their spouses as punch lines. It seems easy and cheap, and a long time ago I simply decided I wouldn't do it, but rather, any time I talked about Dianna, it would be to build her up.

I've seen men talk about their wife as "the old ball and chain," or refer to her as "this one," or "the boss," and if anyone calls them on it, they say, "She knows I love her or I wouldn't tease her." Dianna knows I love her because I say so.

You've challenged your sons that in your family, "We never quit." In what ways has that commitment been necessary?

Life is hard. I know it's a lot harder for people in other countries, and I know it's harder for people who haven't had many of the privileges I've enjoyed. But regardless of success or visibility, the Bible says man is born to trouble as sure as sparks fly upward (Job 5:7).

Like any other family, we've faced trials. I've been unfairly criticized (and sometimes fairly, of course), falsely accused, and the boys have had sports injuries and tough losses, disappointments in love, some seemed to take longer to get through college than the Israelites took to get to the Promised Land, we almost lost one in the recovery room after routine surgery, and the list goes on.

When I was teaching the boys that never-quit principle, it was more about being a good sport. When you're being shellacked on the racquetball court or at table tennis, hopelessly behind, not only do you not concede, but you don't quit playing your best either. Not because you might win—because you probably won't—but because you owe your opponent your best effort. It's the right thing to do.

But that family ethos pays off later when you must endure hardship, serve under an unreasonable boss, take a menial job just to make ends meet, do something you don't want to do for someone else's sake.

You start your book *Hedges* saying the "prudish rules" you have incorporated into your life "are intended to protect my eyes, my heart, my hands, and therefore my marriage." Temptations come in many forms. In what ways have you and Dianna dealt with them over the years, and how does *Hedges* apply today in our "sex-saturated society"?

It shouldn't surprise me, but that book (now in its third incarnation and still in print after twenty-five years) is more needed today that ever. The more prevalent adultery and divorce become among Christians and Christian leaders, the more accepted they seem.

People still see my prohibition against traveling, meeting with, or dining with an unrelated woman alone as prudish, despite all the dangers. I'd like to think I've outgrown the temptations, and I'm fairly certain I'm long past worth anyone risking their reputation for. But I maintain that as one of my hedges for appearances alone, because if you take care of how things look, you take care of how they are. If I'm never alone with an unrelated female, no one can even start a rumor, and if someone simply wanted to ruin my life by making me look bad, my hedge thwarts that.

Of course, nowadays, with pornography a key click away from even children, I don't know how young parents survive without heavy Internet safeguards. Every generation says it gets progressively tougher to raise kids, and this one would be hard to argue with.

Your family has grown from five to fifteen. What impact do your grandchildren, including your adopted grandchildren, now have on you and Dianna?

We've become the quintessential obnoxious grandparents, multimedia shows built into our phones, the whole bit. We would be the grandparents no one can stand, except that our grandkids really are the greatest ever. Just ask.

Our eldest and his wife had three of their own and our second and his wife had two when both couples chose to adopt. First came Max from Bangkok, and that process took so long, it was akin to being pregnant—so the women of the family tell me—for years. Then came Jalen and Chelsea from inner-city Kansas City.

The overwhelming emotion Dianna and I have about all this is that while we have always deeply loved and been proud of our sons and their wives, if they never do anything else as long as they live, adopting these children is enough. Neither they nor we have stars in our eyes about this. We know the challenges—now and likely to come. But that they accepted those as an act of obedience and servanthood could not thrill us more.

What concerns do you have for your family in light of today's accelerating changes and challenges?

It's interesting to me that there was a pocket of ugly racism in my ancestry that somehow my mother overcame—to the point that I was shocked as a teenager to discover it, because she had so well taught her sons the opposite. And our kids are the third of their generation in my extended family to adopt black children, so somewhere there are graves with corpses spinning. And our Christmas card pictures look like the United Nations.

Dianna and I love the look and feel of our family, but we do worry about what our grandkids will face as they grow up. For instance, fair or not (and surely it's not), would my son dare let his black son wear his white brother's hoodie?

For now we love the precious innocence. Our four-year-old black granddaughter kept telling our son at the public pool, "Watch me, Daddy! Daddy, watch this!"

Another girl studied them both and said, "How can he be your dad?"

Chelsea cocked her head, clearly puzzled by the question. "Because he's funny!"

In your books you are quite vulnerable about your strengths and weaknesses. Is that also true in the dynamics of your marriage?

Oh, sure. There's no hiding in the day-to-day of living with someone since 1971. Stephen King has written that one of the secrets to success for a novelist is to marry a woman who doesn't take any [baloney] from you or anyone else. I did that.

What are the best parts now of having been married for so many years?

There's a comfort level in the familiarity. We haven't let each other's quirks become annoying. We know each other's likes and dislikes and habits. We can order for each other. Even though I like spicy foods and she likes mild, I somehow know how much she can tolerate and can tell her whether or not she'll like certain dishes.

We can often communicate with a glance in a crowded room. I still feel as if home is wherever she is, and my favorite journey is back to her. I still like looking at her, and I still get that flutter when she enters a room.

Does Dianna like sports?

She does! And our sons loved that. She would always remind them when ball games were on TV, and we never missed watching them play in youth leagues and in school. She and I still watch a lot of baseball, basketball, and football on TV.

How have you coped with adversity in your marriage?

"This too shall pass," has become a mantra when we face a hard season, but I have to say, we haven't faced the really tough stuff many have. We can't imagine a tragedy in our immediate family. I'd like to think our faith would be strong when really tested.

We live in the Black Forest of Colorado Springs, which was devastated by a fire more than a year ago that took more than 500 homes. We were two intersections south of the worst of it, and only the vagaries of the wind determined whose house was spared. We had friends who lost everything.

I can say, during that week where you didn't know

from one day to the next whether the wind would shift and obliterate everything on your land, that I felt a deep sense of peace. Of course it would have been heart-breaking to lose a repository of so many memories, but everyone was safe. In the end, we told ourselves, the rest of it is just stuff.

PART TWO

4

Where to Live, What to Do . . .

Many would say, "God first, family second, work third." We may believe it and try to live it out, but the truth is that for many of us work consumes the biggest block of our time. Work can be wonderfully absorbing or it can make our lives miserable. The prospect of life after work, retirement, or whatever comes next is both energizing and unsettling. And it all has a profound impact on our marriages.

One wife shared:

> *I've always said, "Work doesn't love you back." My husband took early retirement, and for years we led separate lives, me going off to work every day, him staying home. I started to think, "Is this what I want to do with the rest of my days? What if one of us has declining health?" It's too easy to get caught in a routine and the months turn into years and then suddenly you're seventy and wondering what happened.*

There's that old saying, "Nobody gets to the end and regrets that they didn't spend more time at the office." True, but at the same time, somehow you have to make a living. If you're blessed with absorbing work, and feel like you're making a contribution to the kingdom, and you stay healthy, you may not want to quit entirely. I was able to transition into a more flexible arrangement, which I love.

But we still wonder about the future. I think everyone at our stage does.

In the second half of marriage, few issues are more complex than work: how it's going, when to stop, what to do with ourselves in that alternately scary and inviting "next phase." The drone of media warnings about dire futures for boomers who haven't saved enough for retirement doesn't help. At the same time, many couples are invigorated by the idea of "what's next." It may be a move, a new business, more opportunity for service or travel. Still others aren't so sure about all that "quantity time." One woman we know is typical. Facing retirement after a couple of decades as a social worker, she plans to travel some with her husband for his business. She admits it *could* be interesting, but still, there are many unknowns. Others, especially those with children still in college, keep plugging away well past sixty-five.

So how do we decide? Are there workable answers?

"WE WANT TO BE CLOSE TO OUR KIDS"

Ken and Carolyn are struggling with this issue. He's been a financial planner, a pastor, a writer, and a fund-raiser. She's worked in the family business and now is on staff at a local university. They love their life in Southern California, but Carolyn worries about what happens after she leaves her job. “I do fear what it will be like after I’ve finished working. We live in a very expensive area, but we want to be close to our kids. And we love where we live because it stimulates us. We’re so busy with life right now that it’s scary to talk about and imagine the future.”

Ken laughs. “I’m in total denial about the fact that I’m coming up on age seventy!” He still works and travels as a full-time fund-raiser for a large ministry, but he loves to write and dreams of expanding his side gig into a career. He also dreams of more time with Carolyn.

“We both enjoyed our financial planning business where I worked with clients and Carolyn ran the office. At the same time it’s been fun watching Carolyn come alive in her work at the university. They love her there.”

How might the job negatively affect our marriage? How long can I *do* this job? These are the kind of questions that need to be asked before there is a vocational change.

While Ken celebrates how his wife has come into her own professionally, he is honest about career bumps and bruises. “I reached age fifty-eight and decided I didn’t want to do my business anymore. So I went into ministry, which is what I had studied in college, but it did not end well. Years ago there was a *Time* magazine cover that showed a guy lying facedown on the sand and the cover referred to ‘The Beached White Male.’ That’s what I felt like.”

Ken and Carolyn were forced to move from a beloved six-acre rural property in San Diego County to a smaller place in bustling Orange County. "Our farmhouse was beautiful," Carolyn says. "It was dark and quiet at night. It is not so quiet in our new place. It took us a couple of years to adjust. We reminisced so much that I think it prolonged our sense of loss."

Yet, they realize, God can turn loss into gain.

Ken observes, "I know a man in a wheelchair who says, 'The life I've had I never would have had without this wheelchair.' I think of things that Carolyn and I never would have done had we not had these experiences of loss. It doesn't make the loss easier, but it does balance it out."

THE QUESTIONS WE MUST ASK OURSELVES

The experience of Ken and Carolyn illustrates two of the common realities that many couples face in the second half of marriage. The first is changing vocations. For Ken, this meant closing down his own business and entering a ministry job, which was not a positive experience for him. Carolyn moved from the financial-planning business into working at the university. She had found a vocational change to be a very positive experience. We cannot always predict whether a vocational change will be a positive or negative experience. Of course, we always anticipate the positive.

When contemplating a vocational change, it is extremely important that you learn everything you can about the demands of a new job. Wishful thinking must never be substituted for realistic evaluation. Is this job a fit with my personality and vocational skills? How will this job differ in time requirements from my former job? Will this job require a new lifestyle, for example, does it involve travel? How does the salary compare to my former salary? If it is lower, are we willing to make adjustments in our lifestyle? What potential does this job have for enhancing our marriage? How might the job negatively affect our marriage? How long can I *do* this job? These are the kind of questions that need to be asked before one makes a vocational change.

"The limbo we're in right now has increased our empathy and forbearance for one another."

The second reality that many couples face is changing locations. For Ken and Carolyn, this meant moving from a rural setting to a busy city. Such a move can be traumatic. Sometimes couples choose to change locations in order to be close to their grown children. Often they fail to calculate that their children may also relocate in the next few years. Following our grown children is not always a wise decision.

Again, many questions need to be asked when contemplating a move. How will the move affect us financially? You cannot think only of housing costs but also property taxes. What is our core motivation for moving? Are we ready to give up our long-term friendships in our current location? What is the current mental state of each partner? A depressed spouse may be pushed over the edge by a change in location. Talking to friends your age who have relocated may give you a more realistic picture of the kind of things you might face in making such a transition.

Changing vocations and locations can be extremely positive

for a marriage. On the other hand, they may also be extremely challenging. Such decisions should always be preceded by gaining as much information as you can about the implications of such changes.

"WE TALK AND TALK AND TALK"

So it is for Jane and Rich, who continue to wrestle with the "where-should-we-live" question. Jane tells their story:

> *Some couples slip effortlessly into their retirement years without agonizing over where they'll eventually land. For example, good friends know unequivocally that when they retire, they'll move to the Ozarks, a place they love to consistently visit. For other friends, it was a no-brainer. They bought their dream house in Arizona, then moved there after retiring. That was where they always wanted to be.*
>
> *But I can't say the same for my husband, Rich, and me. Our figuring out this next phase of marriage hasn't been so smooth. In fact, it's been a mix of joy and excitement with confusion and emotion. Ten years ago, we envisioned retirement in a mountain-view log cabin near Durango or Asheville. But now eldercare issues and the birth of grandchildren have entered the equation. So pragmatism has shifted the geography of our dreams to a home in Florida.*
>
> *The truth is, I never wanted to end up in Florida; I'm more a mountains kind of girl. On the other hand, Rich has grown to hate Chicago winters and loves the beach. When his mom entered a Space Coast assisted-living facil-*

ity five years ago, and our first grandchild was born nearby, we started "snowbirding" in Florida. Now it's an annual rite that has triggered plenty of emotion-fraught conversations about whether to transition from "snowbird" to permanent resident.

My husband knows what he wants, but my heart has been conflicted. I long to be near our eldest daughter and her family, yet another daughter, and my parents, still live only a day's drive from our Chicago-area home. Either way, our decision means distancing ourselves from extended family. That's a difficult prospect.

While we want to be close to our children and grandchildren, Rich and I realize we need to choose a path based on what's right for us as a couple. But we also know this: It makes no sense for us to move far away from all family members. So we talk and talk and talk. Rich and I "try on" the various "what-ifs," "whens," and "hows" by walking through them freely and frequently. As we clarify the direction to take at this stage of our lives, we've each moved closer to the other's perspective. Rich wants me to be happy. I want Rich to be happy. We're learning more about each other's hearts, even after thirty-eight years of marriage.

This season, as challenging as it sometimes seems, has opened up important discussions about individual needs and marital goals: personal, familial, and financial. While we may not have started out on the same page, today we're unified in our desire to ultimately find that "happy ending" for each of us. We've not yet staked a Realtor's "For Sale" sign in the front yard of our Chicago home.

"I'M JUST NOT AFRAID"

What if work is painful, even toxic to the soul? Or, what happens when we lose that job?

John and Carole have known the good and the bad over the years: meaningful work with fine colleagues, but also hard and dispiriting days that left them hurting and snappish. Now they're facing John's unemployment.

By their own account, both came from dysfunctional families. Now, as empty nesters, they sometimes think, "Why not split like so many other couples? Why not find happiness elsewhere?" John and Carole didn't. They stuck it out, and now they're still navigating life's turbulence together. How did they get past the roughest patch of their marriage when so many couples give up? How can they face the current challenge of unemployment? One answer may be rooted in the way they handled an unexpected invasion early in their marriage.

"My parents were big fighters," Carole says, "but my mother came back to faith because of Tootie." Tootie was Carole's low-functioning sister with Down syndrome. She and their mother had been rotating living with relatives. Soon after the birth of John and Carole's firstborn, it was their turn to host them. Carole was on maternity leave, and the five of them were cramped in a very small house.

One day her mother asked, "Can we stay?"

As she tells us this story, Carole looks at her husband. "It's a tribute to John that he was so patient with my mom and Tootie, because his father never welcomed extended family."

John was not only patient, he moved the family to a larger

house. The "sacrifices" turned out to include many positives. Tootie lived with them for twenty-five and a half years before passing away. Although she had severe limitations, she was emotionally astute and always ready to lift someone's spirits by singing a song.

"She was actually a whole lot of fun," John says. "We didn't see it as a hardship."

"It was my family, but John stepped up to the plate," says Carole. "Our two boys grew up living with Tootie in her innocence, and knowing their grandmother. They saw it wasn't a perfect world, and that was okay."

John adds, "Tootie influenced the boys. They are compassionate and kindhearted as she was." What could have split their marriage early on instead became a shared purpose and ultimately a bonding force.

John says, "My father was not a loving man. So I didn't know how to respond because I had a bad model." He says he now looks back at ways he could have done better, "but as I look at my wife and children I think, 'I'm doing better than my dad did.' "

"Way better!" Carole asserts.

That includes breaking their parents' patterns during the job turbulence as they held tight to their commitments. They credit their faith as "the essential thing that helped us."

Still, their faith needed bolstering. Recently they found Tim Keller's books and podcasts sparking renewal and drawing them back to "foundations." In times of anxiety, John would say the Lord's Prayer. "Sometimes I wouldn't get past 'Our Father.' I'd think, *Wow! I can call Him Father*, and I'd remember all the Scripture passages that call Him Father."

John said during the job turmoil he thought about what splitting up would be like. Not only did he realize it wasn't going to be better apart from Carole but that their kids needed them to be together. "It would have been a terrible blow to them," he told us. "We made a very serious commitment. Think of it. The vows!"

As a couple enduring the discouragements of job searching, yet getting closer to retirement, they're nevertheless hopeful about the future. "Fifteen years ago, I would have been frightened about this no-job thing," Carole says. "But now, I'm just not afraid."

CELEBRATING YOUR CHOICES

Looking back on your marriage, perhaps you can identify with John and Carole. Perhaps there were unexpected family situations that put extreme pressure on the marriage. You, too, may have entertained thoughts of leaving, but by God's grace you endured those hardships and are still together. Why not take a moment and celebrate that you made good choices in spite of the unexpected circumstances that came your way. One moment of celebration for Karolyn and me was when our son came home from college, put his right hand on my shoulder, his left hand on his mother's shoulder, and said to us, "I want to thank you guys for staying together. I know you had troubles in the early years of your marriage, and I am so glad you stayed together. I have friends at the university who are not going home for Christmas because their parents separated or divorced after they left for college. They don't know which parent to visit for Christmas, so they are staying at the university."

Our hearts responded with sadness for those adult children,

but our son's message to us was extremely encouraging. If you have endured hardship, and yet stayed together long enough to learn how to love, encourage, and support each other, your children also are grateful that you stayed together.

"I STILL DARE TO HOPE"

John and Carole are far from alone in their job struggles. These are the days of underemployment and disappearing jobs, of older workers nudged aside or forced out, losing their sense of identity and security. The search for new work often triggers a long trail of discouragements.

Today's global economic disruptions wreak havoc both in industries and in personal lives. For instance, Alan and Marie are living through the disruption of their many years of long, hard-fought victories over a mountain of debt incurred long ago when Marie went through extensive treatment for cancer. For two decades they've faithfully worked and scrimped to meet their goals of paying off those medical debts. Yet recently, on the verge of getting the loans finally repaid, Alan, who had been at his company for many years, learned his salary was being cut.

It seemed too much to bear. "I was angry," Marie says. "It was very upsetting."

She says of her cancer treatments, "If there's a hell on earth, it was the chemotherapy." A friend who had endured her own treatments had dug a pit at her home for catharsis. "When it was really bad," Marie says, "I broke glass in that pit. When I felt really angry my friend said, 'Okay, we're going to break some glass!' I threw a mayo jar into the pit and it shattered. I found it relieving."

She was still dealing with her sickness when she and Alan experienced new trauma: a son's severe long-term illness and massive hospital and treatment bills. Alan identifies the next eight years as ones of "relentless, exhausting pain. For the longest time it felt like God had pretty much abandoned me and my family."

Then he came across portions of Scripture that made him realize that he could *feel* abandoned by God, yet he could cry out to Him in his pain. Like the psalmist in Psalm 88, he could pray with no need to hide his feelings.

Alan found the same realism in the "weeping prophet." In Lamentations 3 (NLT) Jeremiah complains that God "led me into darkness, shutting out all light . . . I cannot escape . . . He has bound me in heavy chains . . . dragged me off the path and torn me in pieces, leaving me helpless and devastated."

That's not the sort of Bible passage people generally turn to for inspiration! However, Alan resonated with the prophet's anguish and it set him free to express his deepest, pain-filled emotions. He saw the prophet's dark words took a turn into the light: "I will never forget this awful time, as I grieve over my loss," Jeremiah wrote. "Yet I still dare to hope when I remember this: The faithful love of the Lord never ends! His mercies never cease. Great is his faithfulness; his mercies begin afresh each morning."

Alan identified with the prophet's declaration, "I still dare to hope." Identifying with Jeremiah's courage, he keeps hope alive despite his troubles.

Dare to hope. Alan says, "In the throes of darkness, it's remembering God's love and mercies are unending that keeps us going."

Life's troubles continue. Just three weeks before our interview, Alan learned he had been cut to four days a week, at 80 percent of his already reduced salary.

Marie's reaction to this latest reversal was very different from the year before. Like Alan, she digs deeply into spiritual resources, and she finds comfort in remembering that Jesus Himself suffered much and said, "In this world you will have trouble. But take heart! I have overcome the world."[5]

Her first thought in light of the salary cut was to skip their church's end-of-year special offering, since they would have so little. Yet as she prayed about their situation, she felt a fresh peace about contributing.

She says it was as if God were saying to her, "Trust Me."

They've dared to hope for a very long time, in some cases against what seemed medically impossible. Some of those hopes have come wonderfully true. Their two sons are thriving these days, and they're enjoying the blessings of their new daughter-in-law who brings added spark into their family.

RELEASING THE ANGER

Alan and Marie demonstrate the value of the spiritual dimension when we face job loss and financial setbacks. It is so easy to curse the company that treated us unfairly. However, if we spend too much time focusing on the injustice, and allow anger to destroy our well-being, we will miss out on the peace that comes after we share our hurt with God and let Him speak peace to our hearts.

When we lose a job, or are treated unfairly, it is time to look to God for direction. But before we can move forward, we need to release our anger and hurt to God, and trust Him to guide our future. God often uses people, and so we share our need for employment with our friends. We invest our day in looking for work, rather than working. In due time, God will provide. And He will help us grow through the process.

SO HOW *DO* WE PLAN?

With all the joy and pain and stress around the working life, retirement can look pretty good. Right? One wife said, "I heard recently that a couple we've known for over thirty years just entered the 'retirement zone.' The husband is exactly my age. They're actually the first of our peers who are truly, formally retired, not lost-their-job retired or semiretired but still working a little. I thought, 'Would I want to be them and not ever have to worry about work again?'

"Honestly, probably not. But still . . ."

We were chatting with a man age sixty-one who had to be out of work for three months for a knee replacement. He was relieved to finally be back at work and said he was sick of TV and just hanging around.

His wife was sick of it too. "She tells me, 'Go somewhere.' I tell her, 'I'm already in my den, as far away from you as I can get in the house.' She tells me I should go somewhere else, anywhere. 'Why don't *you* go somewhere?' I ask, but she says, 'I was here first.'"

His dilemma reminds us of the man who said this about retirement: "It's twice as much wife, and half as much money."

"We have friends in Florida," the man tells us. "He's been retired two years and his wife tells him, 'You've got to get a job, or a hobby, or *something*.' My financial advisor tells us we could retire now, but there's no way I'm going to."

"I looked at my retiring friends and thought, 'Would I want to be them and never have to work again?'"

But as every one of us with some "seasoning" in life can personally attest, we can't always control what we're going to do or not going to do. Robust health is not guaranteed to us or our spouse. Even the most loyal and effective employee may find herself cut loose. Small businesses go under. Or, as John and Carole found, family shows up on our doorstep.

THREE QUESTIONS

So: To work, or to retire? How do we plan in a world that seems ever less certain? What are the kinds of questions we need to be asking when thinking of retirement?

The fundamental question is, Why do I want to retire? For some, the answer is health issues. They are no longer physically able to work. Others have worked in a very pressured environment, and emotionally are ready to be relieved of such pressure. Others want the freedom to travel, or to play golf every day, or to spend more time with grandchildren. Some desire to spend more time on mission trips, or working in their local church or community. There are good and not-so-good reasons for retiring. However, each couple should seek to honestly answer the question, Why do I want to retire?

Another fundamental question is, What do I plan to do with

my life if I retire? Seek to be realistic in your answers. Some who have retired with the intention of playing golf have told us that after three months they are finding less interest in golf. On the other hand, a friend recently said, "Now that I'm retired, I'm exploring some of the interests I've always had, but never had the time to develop. For example, this semester I'm enrolled in an art class at the local university. I've always wanted to paint, and I'm finding it very exciting." Another friend indicated that he had taken up reading. "There are so many books that I've wanted to read over the years, but have never had time. Now I really enjoy reading. Some days I read in the local library. Others I go to my favorite café. More recently I've been going to the church and finding a quiet place to read. In the summer I sit on a park bench and read. It's really exciting." Our observation is that individuals who retire with specific plans of how they want to use their time usually find retirement enjoyable. On the other hand, those who retire without specific plans often find themselves extremely bored.

We never live long enough to retire from serving God.

The third fundamental question is, Can we afford to retire financially? There is no arbitrary answer as to how many assets one must have in order to retire. However, we suggest that you talk with a financial counselor and let him/her help you assess your financial position. For some, retirement will demand that you change your lifestyle after retirement. Your assets will not allow you to keep living on the same level that you have become accustomed to. Being realistic about your financial assets will help you make wise decisions as you think about retirement.

We believe that man was designed to work. In the beginning God instructed man to work six days a week and rest on the seventh. We find meaning in work when it enhances the lives of our family and others. The theme of life for the Christian is serving God by serving others. Ideally, our vocation should be investing time in a project that is helping humankind. That is why some vocations are not suitable for Christians. Whether we receive a salary for our work, or work as volunteers, we are still working and serving others.

A few years ago, I (Gary) was in Thailand where I met Gary and Evelyn Harthcock, who were in their eighties. They had been there for a number of years teaching English as a second language. Their curriculum had been developed from the Bible. Along with teaching nationals to read, they were sharing the good news of Christ. I asked them, "How do you support yourselves?" He replied, "We receive our Social Security checks and I have a small pension from where I worked, and that's all we need." "How long do you intend to stay here?" I inquired. "As long as we have physical health," he said. "We have no desire to move to Florida, sit in a rocking chair, and wait to die."

I have never forgotten his words. I wish every Christian lived with that attitude. We never live long enough to retire from serving God. Albert Schweitzer invested his life as a medical doctor in what was then French Equatorial Africa. Upon receiving the Nobel Peace Prize, he said, "One thing I know: the only ones among you who will be really happy are those who will have sought and found how to serve."[6]

5

Still Sexual after All These Years

For this chapter we concluded that what might be most helpful would be for Gary to put on his scholar/counselor hat and straight-on address the issue of our sexuality in the later years. Some of the following may be familiar, while other facts and counsel you might find freshly informative. At the end of the chapter you'll find a wish list for making sex better. They just may trigger insights on communicating with your spouse about this important aspect of your marriage.

When we introduced the topic "Still Sexual after All These Years," we received varying responses. One lady said, "Sex, what's that?" While she laughed after asking the question, it made us wonder if sex for her was a thing of the past. Another wife responded, "Better than ever. The children are gone and we are having a ball." One husband said, "The sexual part of the marriage has always been important to us. We had to work hard in the early years to understand the differences between males and females. But in the second half, we are enjoying the fruits of those early efforts." Another husband confessed, "I'll have to admit this has always been a struggle for us, and in the second half we are still struggling." Couples vary greatly in ranking sex as positive, negative, or nonexistent in their relationship.

We believe that, for the Christian, the sexual part of the marriage is extremely important. The Bible speaks clearly on the subject of human sexuality. In the creation account itself, God said, "It is not good for Adam to be alone." God's answer to Adam's aloneness was the creation of Eve, the institution of marriage, and then God said, "The two shall become one flesh." Almost all commentators agree that the term "one flesh" is a primary reference to sexual intercourse. Something happens in sexual intercourse that doesn't happen anywhere else in life. It is not simply the joining of two bodies (you could do that with a handshake). The sexual experience bonds husband and wife together in the deepest possible level: intellectually, emotionally, socially, spiritually, and physically. It is a bonding experience. It is the opposite of being "alone." This is why God reserved sexual intercourse for marriage. It is not a recreational activity between the sexes. It is our unique expression of our love and commitment to each other.

We are often asked, "If sex is so important in marriage, why did God make us so different?" "Why are men stimulated by sight, and women far more by kind words and loving actions?" "Why do men often desire sex more often than their wives?" We believe these and many other differences exist because God intended sex to be an act of love in which each is seeking to bring pleasure to the other. That is why mutual sexual fulfillment does not come automatically. Perhaps this is why God said to ancient Israel, "Take a year for your honeymoon and learn to pleasure each other." If we simply get married and do what comes naturally, we are not likely to find mutual sexual fulfillment. If we make it an act of love in which our attitude is "how can I pleasure you," we will find mutual fulfillment.

Something happens in sexual intercourse that doesn't happen anywhere else in life.

Many couples that struggle in the second half of marriage often struggled in the first half of marriage. The good news is, we are never too old to learn. Many couples have found the second half of marriage to be more fulfilling than the first half. They have learned to communicate more freely, read more books, attend marriage enrichment classes, and in reading the Bible they have discovered that God is very pro-sex in the context of marriage.

God never intended for sex to be put on a shelf after twenty years of marriage. We are sexual creatures as long as we live, and we are to be relating to each other sexually throughout our lifetime. Certainly our bodies change as we get older. Disease can affect us sexually, as can medications. But whatever our limitations, we are still to be reaching out to each other sexually. We are seeking to bring pleasure to each other as we share this intimate aspect of our marriage.

But how are we to keep our sexual relationship vital when we are experiencing the normal physical changes that come with aging? Let's begin by acknowledging that attitude is extremely important. A positive attitude and an openness to communicate our thoughts and feelings as we experience the changes in life is the road that leads to continued sexual intimacy. If, on the other hand, you choose to believe that sex is for the younger years and love is for the latter years, we will rob ourselves and our spouse of sexual intimacy. Let's look at some of the common changes that take place in our bodies as we get older.

MENOPAUSE

Age alone does not limit sexual desire or pleasure. However, menopause will bring physical changes that will impact the female sexually. But the timing of menopause varies with each individual. It may occur anywhere between the ages of thirty-five and seventy, but more typically in the late forties or early fifties.

Menopause is literally a halt, or stop to the menses. This halt is the result of a decrease of hormone production in the ovaries; specifically, estrogen and progesterone. The decrease in estrogen is primarily responsible for most of the physical changes associated with menopause. These changes involve cardiovascular, urogenital, dermatological, skeletal, and neurological systems. The occurrence of hot flashes is easily recognized by women and their partners and serves as harbinger of other changes. Perhaps the most intrusive change for couples that affect sexual intimacy are changes in the urogenital, or reproductive, tract. These changes range from significant vaginal dryness to urinary incontinence to dyspareunia (painful intercourse). Suddenly, a woman may lose interest in sexual intimacy related to discomfort or intense pain. If she in turn withdraws from her partner sexually, he may feel unloved. The physical changes can suddenly cascade into relational changes that were never desired. A husband in frustration may now notice a younger (estrogenized) woman and make unwise decisions with long-term consequences. The importance of communication during menopausal changes cannot be overstated.

Menopause need not mark the end of sexual intimacy. There are medical options to counteract the estrogen drop. Topical estrogen in the form of a cream or pill inserted into the vagina help restore tissue health. Studies on these products find extremely high rates of success, with up to 93 percent of women reporting significant improvement. Between 57 and 75 percent of respondents say their sexual comfort was restored.[7] Or, if you prefer not to go the estrogen supplement route, consider over-the-counter products designed to increase sexual comfort. Long-lasting vaginal moisturizers provide relief from vaginal dryness for up to four days, making intercourse less painful. They have no effect on the underlying cause of vaginal dryness. The wise approach is to talk with your medical doctor about your various options. In our opinion, the worst thing you can do is to simply stop having sex. Open conversation with your spouse and your medical doctor will likely lead you to be able to continue a healthy sexual relationship.

Some women take the attitude that the changes in the body common to menopause simply indicate that this should be the stage in life when you cease to have sexual intercourse. Thus, they are reluctant to turn to medical solutions that offer help. It is interesting to us that those women do not take that form of logic when it comes to other results of an aging body. For example, they are perfectly happy to get glasses when their eyesight begins to dim, or even to have surgery to remove cataracts so that they may continue to see clearly. Why would we accept the benefits of modern medicine when it comes to certain areas of our physical body, but be unwilling to accept the same when it comes to the sexual organs?

ANDROPAUSE

Andropause—sometimes called "male menopause" or Aging Male Syndrome (AMS)—happens at roughly the same time when women experience menopause: sometime between the ages of thirty-five and seventy years, but most commonly in the early fifties. The onset of andropause is stimulated by the decline of hormone levels, in this case testosterone, the male hormone. The decline of testosterone is more gradual in the male than is the sudden drop of estrogen in women who go through menopause. Though hormonal levels diminish gradually, they eventually lead to very real physical effects such as loss of energy, lower sex drive, decreasing strength and endurance, mood changes, and erections that are less strong. While these things may happen, they do not always happen. Many men continue to have a healthy, loving sexual relationship with their wives well into their sixties, seventies, and eighties.

Based on TV ads, one would think that every man over the age of fifty has erectile dysfunction. That is not the case. Technically, erectile dysfunction means that the male cannot raise a semi-firm erection after extended physical stimulation. The majority over age fifty do not suffer from erectile dysfunction. Many men suffer from what is called erectile dissatisfaction. Their erections are not as firm and quick as what they experienced when they were younger, and they become concerned. The fact is that erections do change with the drop of testosterone levels. For some men the process is gradual; for others it happens more quickly. Erections require more physical stimulation, may rise more slowly, and not become as firm as when men were in their thirties and forties. This does not mean that they have erectile dysfunction. Such changes are normal and inevitable. However, some lifestyle factors may postpone or even temporarily reverse these changes. Such things as getting in shape physically, eliminating alcohol and drug abuse, discontinuing smoking, making love earlier in the day when you have more energy, seeking to lessen stress in other areas of life, developing a more positive relationship with your spouse—all may tend to minimize the physical changes that are taking place in your body.[8]

When a wife feels loved by the husband, and the husband feels loved by the wife, it creates an emotional climate in which the two of them can pleasure each other sexually, whatever their limitations.

The slowness of the aging man's sexual response may actually enhance lovemaking. Young couples often have problems because young men become aroused faster than young women. Young men often reach climax before the wife has even started to warm up. Thus, the diminishing level of testosterone slowing down the husband's sexual arousal process, so that his pace more closely matches hers, becomes an asset. A slower pace allows more time for kissing, cuddling, and other affirming touches, all of which are important to the wife's sexual enjoyment.

Some husbands who fail to recognize the difference between

erectile dysfunction and erectile dissatisfaction often turn to the medications they have seen advertised on television, thinking that they will restore their youthful vigor. Most are sadly disappointed. For those men who actually have erectile dysfunction, drugs are worth trying, but don't expect miracles. These drugs improve erections in around two-thirds of men. Even when they do work, it does not take the men back to their youth. It is important to note that these drugs have no effect on arousal. So men may raise erections, but not feel interested in sex. Many men feel disappointed with the results, and fewer than half refill their prescriptions.

So what's a man to do if he finds himself impotent, unable to have or sustain an erection long enough for intercourse? The problem may be compounded if his postmenopausal wife finds intercourse painful, even after trying medical solutions. Most men assume that erections are necessary for sex. The reality is couples can have great sex without intercourse. It is at this stage of life when couples who are relationally healthy learn to give each other sexual pleasure by kissing, cuddling, fondling, massage, and other sexually stimulating touches. In this loving context the wife can still enjoy orgasms and the husband can still reach climax, both of which can be intense and as meaningful as sexual intercourse itself.

Mutual sexual satisfaction does not end with old age. Many times the problems associated with sex in the second half of marriage are not due to lower estrogen and testosterone levels, but rather to the quality of the relationship between the husband and the wife. Sex was never intended to be divorced from the rest of life. That is why understanding your spouse's primary love language and speaking it on a regular basis can keep emotional love alive in your relationship for a lifetime. When a wife feels loved by the husband, and the husband feels loved by the wife, it creates an emotional climate in which the two of them can pleasure each other sexually, whatever their limitations.

To review what we have discussed in chapter 2, the five love languages are: Words of Affirmation, Acts of Service, Gifts, Spending Quality Time, and Physical Touch. If you have not yet discovered each other's primary love language, we highly recommend that you read *The 5 Love Languages: The Secret to Love That Lasts*, and we encourage you to take the love language profile at www.5lovelanguages.com. Increasing the quality of your emotional connection creates the potential of enhancing your sexual relationship.

Communication, which leads to understanding, and love, which motivates one to be open to change, are essential if we are to find mutual sexual satisfaction in the second half of marriage. We have encouraged couples to ask the following questions of each other.

What can we do to help make our sexual relationship better?

What do you wish I would do—or stop doing—to make our sexual relationship better for you?

If I could make one change to enhance our sexual relationship, what would it be?

In the assignment below we are listing some of the answers we received to question number two. We encourage you to read the statements made by others, check those you would like to say to your spouse, add whatever you would like, then sit down and share with each other things you wish your spouse would do, or not do, to make the sexual relationship better for you. Remember your spouse is the expert on himself and herself. Take seriously their requests.

WHAT WIVES WISH THEIR HUSBANDS WOULD DO, OR STOP DOING, THAT WOULD MAKE THEIR SEXUAL RELATIONSHIP BETTER

1. I wish he would take better care of his body so that I would be more physically attracted to him.
2. I wish he knew that things he does throughout the day affect sex that night.
3. I wish he would spend time listening to me without the computer, radio, or television on.
4. I wish he would listen to me and not criticize my thoughts and feelings.
5. I wish he would touch me when he doesn't want sex. Throw a few hugs and kisses in the mix and I would feel more interested in sex.
6. I wish he would let me know that he is proud of me and glad I am his wife.
7. I wish we had consistent date nights without discussing cost—just trying new things together.
8. I wish he would realize that the way he acts after work

or when we're together in the evening (grouchy, impatient, irritable) sets the tone for the night, and I don't have a switch that turns all of that off and suddenly makes me want to have sex with him.

9. I wish my husband would remember that intercourse is painful for me (postmenopausal). I want to please him because I love him very much.
10. I wish that he would understand that my lack of interest has nothing to do with him. It has everything to do with my lack of time, energy, and my stress level.
11. I wish he would work with me on our spiritual relationship.
12. I wish my spouse would seek help for impotency. It has been an issue for years.

WHAT HUSBANDS WISH THEIR WIVES WOULD DO, OR STOP DOING, THAT WOULD MAKE THEIR SEXUAL RELATIONSHIP BETTER

1. I wish she would join me in an exercise program.
2. I wish my wife would initiate sex more often. It is measurably more enjoyable for me when she is more active in getting things started.
3. I wish she would open up more and talk about this part of our marriage.
4. I wish there could be some variety in our sexual relationship, and that it would happen more often.
5. I wish we had sex more than once a year. I wish that her mind was on me rather than her family (her mom and

dad). Maybe when they die we can have sex.

6. I wish my wife saw it more as a mutual experience. It seems more and more about meeting my needs, rather than an exciting experience for us.
7. I wish she would allow herself to let go of past experiences and enjoy our sexual relationship.
8. I wish my wife would seek medical advice for a physical problem she has that makes it painful for her to have sex. I'm frustrated and don't know why she won't seek help.
9. Over the years her lingerie closet has become fuller, but is opened less often. She is a beautiful woman and I would enjoy seeing her open the closet more often.
10. I wish she would stay awake when we are making love. Her pleasure is just as important as mine, and it's not fun for me when I am making love with someone who's not even conscious.
11. I wish we could dedicate more time to our physical relationship. I wish she understood the importance of it. I miss the closeness.
12. I wish my wife would allow me to pleasure her sexually. She has a general attitude that sex is "nasty." I know she was sexually abused as a child, but she refuses to go for counseling.
13. I wish she would make suggestions to me on what makes the sexual experience more pleasurable for her.

6

Do Not Be Anxious?

There's anxiety. Then there's worry. Then there's stark, raw fear.

And all of them are regular visitors to many of us, usually in the middle of the night. *Will my cancer come back? Will we be able to afford to stay in our house? What happens to our not-fully-functioning son? Did I just hear something?*

Many of us in marriage's second half find much to be happy about. We're not alone. We have a partner. We've endured significant losses and know we're survivors. We have food, shelter, family, and friends. To at least some degree, we understand the new research saying people get happier as they age.

Well, up to a point. As one couple said, "In the first half of our marriage, we had stress about paying for a car, a house, and dealing with our kids, but we were not fearful. Now we are fearful about: our energy levels, that we'll run out of money, that we'll lose our health, or go into cognitive decline."

Debt among Americans age fifty-five and older keeps climbing. As we've seen, many couples have been hit hard by corporate downsizing while others wonder if they can hold on to their jobs. Among the retired, one couple said, "We can't believe how much it costs to be on Medicare, all the premiums, and the co-pays. We saved all our working lives, but unless we can die sooner rather than later, we'll run out of money." Yet whatever their ages, from the fifties on up, these couples affirmed their appreciation of each other and their general sense of well-being. One said, "The awareness of all that could happen is always there, but we try to live in the moment, with thankfulness for what's good."

That's not always easy.

As creatures susceptible to disease, accidents, mental breakdowns, and other ills, we have more than enough to worry about. It's the human condition. Unfortunately our culture ramps up our anxieties, flooding us with sobering information and vivid images of terrible things in the world. Amy Simpson, in her book *Anxious,* reports that many of us are "frantic with worry. Worry is part of our culture." She found that "the unknown future" is the number-one source of worry.

"YOU CAN FEEL GUILTY FOR FRETTING"

This is where faith comes in.

Jesus had a lot to say about worry, and He said it to His closest friends. In fact, His statements are so practical they resonate with the best of today's behavioral studies.

After warning against greed and describing a rich farmer confident he could retire in comfort and luxury, Jesus called him a fool. Death, after all, comes to even those with heavily funded retirement plans. Then He turned to His friends and gave them this no-nonsense advice: "Do not worry about your life, what you will eat or drink; or about your body, what you will wear. Is not life more than food, and the body more than clothes?"

He asked, "Who of you by worrying can add a single hour to his life?"

The truth is, we all know that worrying can do the opposite—*take* hours from our lives, releasing inflammatory proteins and compromising our immune systems.

"Unless we can die sooner rather than later, we'll run out of money."

After urging His disciples to consider the birds, who do not fly around worrying, Jesus shared this spiritual and psychological advice: "Do not worry about tomorrow, for tomorrow will worry about itself. Each day has enough trouble of its own."

True enough! In fact, each day's troubles can be far more than enough. "It's hard NOT to worry about the unknown future," says Laura. "I survived cancer, and so far, I am doing okay, but who knows about the next several years? My husband has back problems. What if he becomes a cripple? You don't know how long you're going to live, or what quality of life you're going to have. You don't know if your money will run out. We've thought about moving to live near our kids, but we're not sure where they're going to live.

"There are a lot of unknowns at this stage, especially when you're in your sixties and just looking out at the future. It's worse when you have an overactive imagination, like I do! At the same time you can feel guilty for fretting, because at the end of the day you have got to trust in God who holds the future."

WORRYING AND PRAYING

As Laura (and all of us) have experienced, we cannot keep the mind from contemplating the future. In fact, it's healthy to think about the future. Such thoughts should lead us to make plans for the future. It's difficult to think about, but one reality for all of us is death. I (Gary) once said to my daughter, who is a physician, "If something happens to me . . . " She replied, "No, Dad, not if, but when you die." I said, "Yes, when I die . . . "

The reality of death should lead us to prepare for death, spiritually and financially. Where will you be buried, and how will your spouse pay the expenses?

We cannot control all of the events that will happen in our future. We must trust God to give us grace and wisdom to face those events when they happen.

Thinking about the future should lead us to take constructive steps to prepare for the future. But good plans are not enough. We must also trust God. We cannot control all of the events that will happen in our future. We must trust God to give us grace and wisdom to face those events when they happen.

We have all heard people say, "I don't know how I can go on living if my spouse dies." This attitude focuses on the loss rather than on God. We don't need grace to face the death of a spouse until the spouse dies. God will be there on that day as He is with you today. I once heard a pastor say, "God does not give 'dying grace' on non-dying days." Trusting God is the antidote to worry.

Worry is an enemy. Worry is our mental response to what "might" happen. The word *worry* means "to be torn apart." Worry is different from concern. Concern leads to action. Worry ultimately leads to hopelessness. As Christians we are challenged not to worry but to pray. Worry focuses on the situation and what might happen. Prayer focuses on God and His power to help us.

Someone who really got this message was famed physician Sir William Osler, who shared his insights at Yale University in 1871. He urged the students to begin their days with Christ's prayer, "Give us this day our *daily* bread."

Osler told of traveling on an ocean liner on which the captain could order that various parts of the ship be separated from one another into watertight compartments. It struck a chord with the busy doctor. Osler determined to cultivate the habit of living in "day-tight compartments," and in his speech he advised the students to live each day without worrying about either past or future.

His speech has been widely quoted, and many have found his mental image helpful: live in day-tight compartments. Work on preparations for the future, but as part of the day's tasks.

More ideas: *Recognize the power of your thoughts.*

The capacity of the mind is awesome. For instance, when you're feeling down, deliberately put a smile on your face. It actually changes your body chemistry. Try it! Paul the apostle also writes about the power of positive thoughts as an anecdote for worry (Philippians 4:8).

Accept what is.

Some things seem impossible to accept. Yet brooding over them, living in denial or anger generates dissonance. We must accept reality.

Decide what action you can take. "Part of the problem with worry is, it's so unproductive," says a friend of ours. We can't change the future. But perhaps we can do something to improve the situation. There's nothing worse than feeling paralyzed. Even a small step is better than no step

Consider Mark Twain's comment.

The writer said he'd had many troubles in life, but most of them never happened. We can mentally paint scenarios of all the bad things that may happen to us, but only a few actually do.

Don't beat yourself up.

Sometimes we just can't get over bad decisions made, or lost opportunities. However, the longer we focus on the past, the less time we have to make a better future. Accept what was and is, and let go of regrets.

And again . . . *pray.*

A husband told us he was finding some success in his prayer life, and that has lessened his anxieties. Here's what he said:

My wife and I have lots of worries about our kids, grandkids, and finances. In addition, the stupid and sensual stuff on TV, and my phone, and in magazines mix in my brain with all the horrific news clips. But I've been trying something in my prayer life that's been helping. It's simple. It short-circuits my turmoil and dread, at any time of day.

I think of one person; let's say it's Joe, and I simply pray, "Bless Joe."

That's it. One at a time, starting with my wife and family, I let names and faces flow through my mind, and for each of them I simply pray, "Bless Jane. Bless Mario," and move on to many more.

I once read a book on the power of a parent's blessing a child. The child absorbs the love and gains a sense of identity. The word "bless" has power. As I pray just those two words of blessing on names and faces, it reminds me of the Lord's Prayer asking that God's will in heaven be brought to earth.

I feel a change in chemistry when I ask God to bless my loved ones, and people who are a mess, or people who have hurt me. "Bless" means I'm asking God to pour His oil of love and redemption on that person. As I pray name after name after name, those news clips and enticements fade. I'm asking God to bring heaven and His holy love to these people. My own problems seem less worrisome.

I can't fix this world or all our troubles. But when I pray this way, I'm saying I'm trusting God for what's really important—people. Because I allow my mind to wander from person to person as I pray, I find I've soon prayed for lots of people, some I haven't seen in years. It's caused me to reach out to some I've been avoiding.

Yes, sincere prayer is a ministry to others, and it keeps our focus on God rather than our circumstances.

The story is told of J. C. Penney, the founder of the chain of stores that bear his name, that after the financial crash of 1929, he was so worried he couldn't sleep. "I was broken nervously and physically, filled with despair." One night he awoke convinced it was the last night of his life. He got out of bed to write letters to his wife and son, saying he did not expect to see the dawn.

Next morning, he awoke still alive. "I heard singing in a little chapel where devotional exercises were held each morning. They were singing, 'God will take care of you.'"

The effect on him was profound. He said, "I listened with a weary heart to the singing, the reading of the Scripture lesson, and the prayer. Suddenly, something happened. I can't explain it. I can only call it a miracle. I felt as if I had been instantly lifted out of the darkness of a dungeon into warm, brilliant sunlight. I felt the power of God as I had never felt it before. I knew that God's love was there to help me. From that day to this, my life has been free from worry. I am seventy-one years old, and the most dramatic and glorious twenty minutes of my life were those I spent in that chapel that morning: 'God will take care of you.'"

MAKING IT PERSONAL

Philippians 4:6–7: "Do not be anxious about anything, but in everything, by prayer and petition, with thanksgiving, present your requests to God. And the peace of God, which transcends all understanding, will guard your hearts and your minds in Christ Jesus."

When we put our concerns in the hands of God, there is no further need for worry.

1. What do you most often worry about?
2. Can you think of anything you might do to address your concerns? If so, why not take those actions.
3. In the verses above, we are instructed to pray, make requests of God, and then thank Him that He loves us, and will help us cope with whatever happens. We put

our concerns in His hands and trust Him. The result is peace, which is the opposite of worry.

4. If you feel overwhelmed and hopeless, then perhaps the one thing you can do after you pray is to share your pain with a trusted friend, pastor, or counselor. God often uses people as His helpers.

Joni and Ken Tada

"TO KNOW EACH OTHER LIKE THE BACKS OF OUR HANDS"

JONI EARECKSON TADA *is well known for her powerful insights on suffering, her artistic gifts, and her worldwide ministry, Joni and Friends. But she has also written extensively on marriage, specifically her thirty-four years of marriage to husband (and ministry partner), Ken. Her latest book,* Joni & Ken, *reflects on those years of a "hard-won union." She shared some of her counsel, and her joy, with us.*

You've said we live in a society that doesn't know what to do with suffering, that we try to escape it, and "marriage only magnifies it." What can strengthen a marriage in times of suffering?

When suffering sinks its jaws into your marriage, thrashing it violently, it's all you can do to hold on. But, if you can hold on to vows, and to Christ through the worst of it—violent emotions or splintered circumstances—your marriage will be stronger for it. To hold on is to reach for those "disciplines" that, in the past, have seen you through tough times: praying for each other, and staying in the Word.

But through it all, *pray*. Whenever Ken gets in a funk, or shuffles around the house with a sour disposition, I pull aside and privately pray for him. I plead before the throne for him, asking God to remember His servant; to pour out grace upon him; to help him defeat sin; to open his eyes to the Big Picture; to apply every benefit of the resurrection to my husband, and more. It's amazing; my husband responds very, very well to prayer.

The cover of your 1986 book, *Choices/Changes,* shows you and Ken looking into the camera brightly happy, like two young newlyweds. Your new book cover shows you starkly different, like two seasoned veterans, gritty survivors. As you think about these photos, what goes through your mind and spirit?

What a telling observation, and I have thought the same about those covers. I would never, ever want to go back to that youthful, idealistic, and romantic stage of our marriage. Oh, how much I, how much Ken and I, prefer this stage: to know each other like the backs of our hands, to prefer his quiet company over any noisy pursuit; to enjoy the utter comfort of his friendship; to recognize each painful notch in our scraped and scuffed belts as evidence of growing closer to God and to each other; and, to be home with each other. Home is where Ken is. And I am home for him.

You refer to the necessity of "a hard-fought, hard-won union with your spouse." You emphasize, "Oh, please *pray* for your partner. Hands down, it beats any how-to marriage manual." What makes you say this?

There are seasons when you will not like the person you married. You'll despise his laziness and long hours on the couch, flipping through fishing magazines; his accumulating stuff, his belching and love of beach walkers worn *everywhere*. You'll resent that energetic, engaged tone of voice he shows with his guy friends, leaving you with "yeah," "nah," and the occasional grunt. When those seasons happen, remind yourself that there is *no other person in the world as important as he:* no girlfriend, no mentor, no coworker, no spiritual parent, no neighbor or other relative, not even your father and mother is as important as this person. Of all the things or people in the world to pray for, *this person* tops the list. He is the one to whom you have vowed to love for better or for worse. You have a solemn obligation to get engaged in your spouse's sanctification through prayer. He's the person God put in your life to pray for, cheer on, defend, encourage, appreciate, and applaud. To love him in such a way even does *your* soul a *world* of good!

Many find it remarkable you can praise and be thankful considering the extreme crosses you've borne. How has a sense of gratitude affected your marriage?

We are not creatures of gratitude, naturally. And I'm sure that's why God tells us time and again to be thankful. We may not feel inclined to thank our spouse for things, because we are too busy monitoring his bad behavior ("Has he earned my thanks? Has he done anything lately to warrant my gratitude?"). But come on, really, surely, *certainly* there is "some small redeemable quality" in your spouse; some tiny Christlike characteristic you can nurture, you can encourage with words of thanks! (I'm not talking about empty flattery that manipulates. I'm talking about nurturing a Christlike attribute.) When you express gratitude and appreciation, you are partnering with the Holy Spirit in "growing" admirable and godly attributes in the other. So if you don't have a spirit of gratitude, start working on it. As you do, the person God may change in your marriage is both of you.

When you were diagnosed with cancer, you said to Ken you believed it had come "with great purpose" and that "God must be up to something." With all you and Ken have endured over the years, how have you seen "purpose" in your marriage?

One of the most telling qualities of suffering is its ability to refine: to hone and shape and polish (assuming that we humble ourselves and yield to its purposes). Affliction, physical pain, loss, and near-death experiences strip away the frivolous and superfluous in marriage, leaving us at times nearly decimated. But stripped to the basics, Ken and I have more easily recognized the Big Picture. Our purpose is to honor God by keeping our vows. We want to be a couple that models what it means to submit and yield, lead and guide, confess and forgive, listen and talk, work and play, care and correct, and every other action verb that contributes to the joy and richness of life. Our goal in marriage is to strive to be each other's best friend, the one whom the other chooses, prefers, boasts of, defers to, brags about, defends, and at night falls into bed with, feeling safe and secure. There's *nothing* sweeter in the world.

One chapter in your book is titled, "It's Not about Us." What do you mean by that?

Honestly, we want to finish well. We don't want to do anything in our marriage that would embarrass Jesus, or make Him look bad, smear His reputation or displease Him. There's a *wide* gap between what you would naturally do (like whine about your spouse) *and* what you do by God's grace (like biting your tongue from grumbling, and instead, praying for him). That gap is the glory of God. That gap, that "difference" between complaining and choosing *not* to complain, makes God look great!

Are you and Ken opposites?

Yes, we are opposites. But we are both competitive athletes. Nothing's more fun than being with Ken in front of an HDTV, an NCAA game, and a bowl of chips and Ortega salsa. I also love it when my husband cracks up at something so hard, that he starts laughing at himself. His silly humor used to bug me, but not anymore. We have a Japanese minion on our refrigerator with wok in hand, insane grin, bucked teeth, and the rest. A thing like that would have made me fume years ago. But now, I love his silly sense of humor.

You and Ken are strong individuals. Ken has certainly fought fierce battles in partnership with you. How has his masculine "warrior" side and your powerful leadership drives become complementary rather than divisive? Has that been difficult?

We both compete to win. We remember the Big Picture. We're energized by challenges. Most importantly, we recognize that every day God calls us onto a fierce battlefield upon which the mightiest forces in the universe converge in warfare. That invigorates us! Our enemy is not my wheelchair, or my pain, or my quadriplegia. It's Satan. He'll do anything to lob hand grenades into our relationship. Ken Tada and I are both pretty much aware of that, and so, remain vigilant. I think the disability helps that.

With the changes in men's and women's once-traditional roles now a fact of life for so many, what do you see as essential to a thriving marriage?

Somebody's got to have the last say. I mean, we can mutually submit all we want, but when push comes to shove, when a decision is needed, we abide by Ken's call. And I have to trust the Lord that even if I feel it is the wrong call, we're doing the right thing. And because of that, I believe God will protect us and move us forward.

How have you been able to be so forthright about your struggles and experiences? How can other couples engage honestly with each other when harsh realities invade?

Ken and I spend a lot of time at our Joni and Friends Family Retreats. We meet couples holding on by a thread, trying valiantly to keep love alive while raising three kids, two with serious autism and maybe the other with Down syndrome. Ken and I look at them and say, "We don't know *nothing.*" Part of the reason we stay so transparent and vulnerable is because we want to show these couples that they can make it, that we resonate with their struggle, and that Jesus can pull them through. Spending time at our Family Retreats keeps us "close to the ground" where most of the world lives. When harsh realities invade, a couple can engage each other by simply listening, asking a few probing questions, then listening and "just" listening.

I think most of us are *dying* for our spouse to just

listen to us: to understand us, to "get" us, and to still keep loving us.

There's a message out there in the culture that staying married is impossible for the vast majority and that serial monogamy is the best couples can hope for. How do you respond to that? And what would you say to those who have had it with their marriages and are ready to break up?

A Christian *can* break marital ties with his or her spouse. Life will go on, and you may find some happiness down the road with another; but you *will not be* the same person. You will not be the "you" you deeply and desperately want to be. You will be lesser a man, a woman, diminished. Although it is true that genuine repentance will bring restoration (oh, how *amazing* the grace of God!), your soul's capacities will be less. (I mean that word "capacities" as Jonathan Edwards spoke of it. Habitual sin has a way of diminishing the Christian vessel. Once forgiven we can still experience an overflow of God's grace and joy, but the vessel will be smaller. I think this is what Jesus was speaking about when He warned His followers that they could risk being called "least in the kingdom of heaven" if they chose a sinful path. Are the cosmic stakes really *that* high? Yes they are! This isn't a teaching against grace, it shows grace to be precious, not cheap. It is a teaching much needed in the church today.)

We've found many long-married couples struggle with anxiety about what's ahead. You've had more than enough health reasons to feel anxious, and you've taken needed medications that induced anxiety. How do you and Ken deal with anxiety when it arises?

Funny you should ask. This past Sunday was Communion, and as I contemplated sin that needed to be confessed, "fear of the future" jumped out in front: *I wonder if I can handle much more physical pain? What will I do if Ken Tada dies before me? If I should become bedridden, will I be able to gracefully accept it?* Mine is a constant fight to stay content right here, right now, and quit worrying about "tomorrow and whether or not my corset will be digging into me." My constant inspiration is the prophet Samuel who, after he raised his memorial, said, "Thus far the Lord has helped us!" He has met every need, more than abundantly. And I have absolutely *no reason* to think (this is where the fight kicks in) that He will fail me in the future.

With your heavy travel schedule and the weight of your leadership responsibilities, how do you continue to keep your marriage positive?

I am exceedingly blessed that Ken Tada feels that Joni and Friends is something we do *together*. He travels with me on virtually every trip (unless he's fly-fishing in Montana), and we enjoy it immensely. I keep telling him, "Honey, you don't *have* to go on every trip," but he wants to! We enjoy speaking together. He hands out "Joni's

Story" gospel tracts to every flight attendant, skycap, flight supervisor, hotel clerk, hotel maid, busboy, waitress, and the rest. Nothing makes me more proud than to hear him encourage these people to read my story.

Our marriage is a positive experience because we both see how God is using us in His kingdom. In fact, when we are tired or bored, we will recount over dinner all the amazing places we've been in more than fifty countries; we'll recount the people, the blessings, the opportunities, the marriages rescued, the depression lifted, the sights seen, and so much more. We are very blessed. Very.

PART THREE

7

Resilient Together

Bouncing back. Rising above. Coming through.

Whatever you call it, this quality can make *all* the difference in a successful marriage. How do some couples survive natural disasters, business failures, and all kinds of trauma, while other marriages do not survive? How do some people—like Joni and Ken Tada—cope with chronic health conditions with grace and even humor, while others give in to bitterness and passivity?

Of course the answers are many and complex. But there is great healing power in simply going through something *together*.

Barb and Jim were looking forward to the inheritance they knew they would be receiving from his widowed mother someday. She had always lived frugally and amassed a sizable estate. But when she developed dementia, Jim's brother Dave stepped in to manage her affairs. "Between some bad investments he made and the worldwide economic crisis, she lost almost everything," Barb said. "Plus we took our eye off the ball, to be honest. Dave did not communicate much and by the time we got an eldercare attorney involved, it was really too late. We're just grateful that she never knew what happened to the money she had so painstakingly saved."

Barb could have blamed Jim for not paying closer attention to Dave, who had a history of unwise financial dealings. She didn't! "Look, I didn't pay attention either. At the time we were in the middle of moving ourselves, as well as looking at places for Jim's mom. Our kids had needs. Eventually, Jim did step in and take control away from his brother.

"We were in it together. And as Christians we didn't want to be divided over issues of money. We're a team, and that's that." She added that it has helped that their overall financial picture is reasonably healthy. "We're not broke, but yeah, the inheritance would have helped, a lot. But my relationship with Jim is everything, and a right perspective on *life* is everything.

"I think we learned a lot from the whole ordeal."

"THE GRIEF AND PAIN SEEMED TO GO ON AND ON"

The resilience of a marriage depends on many things. When resilience cracks and a marriage is in trouble, spouses often hurl angry accusations. Anger can perk quietly in a marriage month after month, ready to spill over and scald. Scripture tells us, "In your anger do not sin." Putting that into practice is far from simple. Repressed anger results in depression, yet expressing or acting on it can wound and scar.

Anger turned on a spouse can be irrational, and one man described an incident showing just that. "It was crazy," he said. "One night, I got up to use the bathroom and stubbed my toe.

It hurt! My anger flared, and instantly rushing through my head was, 'It's her fault!!!' Yet she had nothing to do with it."

This husband rejected his irrational thought, but pain or loss often crowd out the rational. When anger festers or flares, a spouse can become a target.

We liked what we heard from Michael and Andrea about handling anger. They've experienced more than their share of anger-inducing sorrow and suffering. When he lost his job with a major corporation and was unemployed for nearly a year, Michael was angry for a long time. "I took perverse delight at hearing bad news about the company that had let me go."

As a couple, they say they've had a model for handling anger, the faith of Michael's father. "My dad struggled with anger issues. He lost his mother when he was three and his father when he was seven. When my dad was only twenty-eight, he was diagnosed with terminal melanoma. He thought, 'Here we go again.' He wasn't ready to die. My sister and I were little. Dad pleaded with God to let him live to raise his children. Shortly thereafter, Dad participated in an experimental treatment in New Orleans, and it worked. He was cancer-free for a very long time."

When calamities come, it can be hard to remember all those marriage-enrichment attitudes we're supposed to display.

Much later in his dad's life the cancer returned, with devastating results. But Andrea says, "He now has an amazing attitude. He insists he's okay and says, 'God knows what He is doing in my life. I'm fine.' He is a remarkable testament to faith."

His father's example was one reason Michael stayed relatively calm when Andrea called him one day in a panic. It was a few days before Christmas, and their daughter, Anna, home from college, was cleaning the bathroom. "She's a deep cleaner," Andrea says, "and she decided to clean the grout. She started to pull it away, and suddenly the filth of the universe tumbled from the walls into the bathtub."

Anna screamed. "Mom, there are worms coming out!" Andrea rushed to the bathroom and saw termites spilling out and writhing in the tub.

Michael drove home and tried to calm her down, but his calm did not influence her. She wanted to leave their house, but he didn't see the termite infestation as that serious a problem. Michael was thinking, "Maybe she'll realize life isn't over."

"I was angry at what was happening," she says, "and angry that Michael couldn't wave a magic wand to make it better. He made me furious."

When calamities come, it can be hard to remember all those marriage-enrichment attitudes we're supposed to display.

How bad was the infestation? Later they learned there's a stage when termites are called "swarmers" and develop wings. Andrea experienced them up close and personal. "I wanted to see what was back there, so I took a sledgehammer and tapped out a tile. Suddenly swarmers were flying around everywhere in the bathroom."

Despite all that, Michael's dry sense of humor prevailed. He said, "I wonder how they would taste if we deep-fried them." Andrea said, "That was the turning point. No matter what happens, he turns it into humor—even with those termites. We both laughed, even though we knew we had a serious problem." The termites cost them many thousands of dollars and made their house unsellable. Andrea became very sick from the exterminators' poisons, but they survived. Sometimes laughter breaks the cycle of the fear and anger.

That was not the last chapter of stress, fear, and anger for Michael and Andrea. A few years later their daughter, Anna, now out of college and married, became pregnant. They were overjoyed, but she had problems and was often hospitalized. One day they found themselves with Anna and her husband, listening to a doctor explaining that Anna's amniotic fluid was gone. On the ultrasound they saw a perfectly formed little boy, but they were told he would not survive.

The next day they induced labor. "It was awful," Andrea remembers. "The happy pictures of babies were taken off the hospital walls and a yellow rose taped to the door so nurses would know what was happening. The grief and pain seemed to go on and on."

Later, Anna again became pregnant. Joy swelled, but soon gave way to pain. Anna was experiencing the same problem: bleeding and loss of amniotic fluid. This new little boy was not going to make it.

Andrea recalls her thoughts: "'She cannot go through this same thing again.' I was so angry!"

For Michael, the second miscarriage was the more painful. "It seemed cruel." And he flared at a doctor's simply saying, "Well, this happens and it could happen again."

WHY?

Accepting what happens in life is a huge challenge for all of us. Babies die and doctors may seem brusque. Accidents devastate families. Alzheimer's steals a once-sparkling mind. Worldwide, innocent children are trapped in human slavery and terrorized by violence. Why did Anna lose two babies? Why, Lord?

Many wise thinkers from the great religious traditions have sought to wrestle with the question that has haunted mankind since Job. Why? But even when we have our theology well formed, we still must deal with our human responses to grief, bewilderment, and anger.

As couples, when we are able to act in love, whatever our pain, we are better able to enjoy the wonders of life. For Michael and Andrea, a new wonder powerfully graced their lives.

Late one night Andrea received a text from Anna about a doctor who had developed a new technique. Babies of women with problems like Anna's were surviving.

They visited the surgeon, who assured her that she and her husband could become parents.

Anna had the surgery. But her regular doctors, unfamiliar with the process, expected it to fail. During her pregnancy, Anna was in and out of the hospital, with lots of bed rest at her parents' home.

"I was afraid for her," Andrea says, "but we prayed and hoped. I kept reading the testimonials of all the women who had babies because of the surgery."

Baby Ruby, a five-pound girl, now laughs and smiles constantly, and has a large Facebook following. Andrea credits prayer. "I believe our church prayed Ruby into existence."

Although Andrea and Michael were angry during the losses. "I was trying not to be angry at God. For a time, I just stopped praying. I didn't want to be crying out to God when others were enduring even worse things. There was so much suffering everywhere and I eventually asked, 'Why not me?'" Michael and Andrea's faith and love for each other kept them walking together!

WHEN ROLES CHANGE

As we get older, we wonder what health problems we'll endure, and how we'll deal with them. We've been inspired by couples with serious health issues who are determined to live with purpose and grit.

As we age, the core of who we are doesn't change, and what we can no longer do shouldn't define us.

Vic and Betsey struggle with his Parkinson's, which limits Vic in frustrating ways. It's tough for Betsey as caregiver, and it's tough for Vic as he loses his skills and self-reliance. "It can seem she's always telling me what to do," Vic says.

"It's a male thing," he says, explaining his feelings of resistance and loss when she helps him with his pills. "Betsey questions my ability, taking tasks out of my hands."

Yet Vic knows she has to step up to do what must be done, and Betsey says it takes patience and grace for both of them.

He compliments her: "You've developed ways to deal with me."

"And you with me!" she responds.

Evident are the benefits of a long marriage with a history of mutual respect and give-and-take as they talk about working through changed roles and tensions. Generally, as we age, the core of who we are doesn't change, and what we can no longer do shouldn't define us. Instead of grumbling that Vic has difficulty putting on his coat, they've focused on what they do have: wonderful children and grandchildren, and each other.

"Having gratitude," Betsey says, "is an attitude of life. It changes everything! It changes how we look at Parkinson's. We've never once asked, 'Why us?' We've had all these years together. He's still alive and warm. We're partners, no matter what."

THROUGH THE FIRE

Carl and Lanette work together in their small truck-parts business. One day they were at work when they heard someone yell that an apartment in one of the buildings attached to their business was on fire. "Smoke was coming from a window," Carl remembers. "I ran in and pounded on all the doors, yelling for people to get out. With fire trucks on the way, we grabbed tarps to protect against water damage and removed all the computers."

A fire engine shot its thousand gallons of water into the burning apartment. Two firemen went in and waited for more water. "For fifty years, we'd had a discount on our fire insurance since we were close to a hydrant," says Carl. "But it was dry! There was no water at all. They tried a different one a few blocks away, but it was dry too."

A third hydrant produced some water, but not enough. Horns blew signaling the firemen to get out, and seven hours later most of the buildings were gone. After decades of effort to build their business, the couple watched it go up in smoke.

This is the sort of moment couples can be plunged into

despair, or voice recriminations, or lash out at someone. But Carl and Lanette resisted suggestions they sue. They also rejected the temptation to be bitter about a competitor taking advantage of the fire by trying to steal their customers. Instead, they concentrated on expressing gratitude for kindnesses shown and for those who helped them keep their business alive. A customer sent in $500 for future parts, knowing they would need cash; suppliers extended terms. Best of all, a major competitor called and said, "Carl, I really feel bad about your fire. To help you get back on your feet, I'm going to send one of my trucks to you every day with whatever parts you need to stay in business."

What a gift, and what a reason to feel gratitude!

"I LEARNED I HAD TO BE TAKEN CARE OF"

The fire wasn't the only crisis the two endured. Carl suffered a compound fracture requiring three surgeries. The accident happened as he was helping his son build his house. On the porch, he climbed a ladder and shot a nail gun to fasten a shingle. At that instant, something flew off and hit him in the face. He thought it was a nail, but it was an alarmed bat. It flew right at him and startled him.

Carl fell, but his foot caught between the rungs of the fiberglass stepladder.

As he lay by the wet concrete, he looked at his foot. Two bones were sticking out. Suddenly he felt intense pain.

The ambulance came. Carl's vital signs dipped dangerously low. At the hospital six screws and two plates were required to repair his foot.

"It was quite an ordeal," he says, "and it's hard to get it out of your head. When it happened, our three-year-old granddaughter, Rachel, was right there with me, and she was scared to death. It was several months before she would come anywhere near me."

"Instead of saying, 'You're wrong,' we learned to say, 'You might be right.'"

Carl views the experience as a turning point. "I learned I wasn't self-sufficient; that sometimes I needed care. I learned to say, '*The Lord willing* I'll do something.' I learned to be grateful that Lanette was taking care of me."

"We all go through these kinds of things," Lanette added. "We just have to stay faithful and deal with what's happened."

At a Marriage Enrichment weekend, they talked honestly about their struggles. Lanette gave an illustration: "We learned something really important. Instead of saying, 'You're wrong,' we learned to say, 'You might be right.' Nobody wants to be wrong. So many times in so many situations, we've said, 'You might be right!'"

Carl concurred. "And sometimes later we have to say, 'You actually *were* right.'"

SEVEN SECRETS OF RESILIENCE

These stories of real people have brought us to the following conclusions:

1. All couples will face difficulties.
2. When we focus on solving the problem, rather than

blaming each other, we are more likely to find a solution.

3. We cannot change circumstances, but we can change our attitude. A positive attitude always wins.
4. We will not always understand why things happen. The question is not, "Why did this happen to us?" but rather, "What can we learn from this experience?"
5. Turning to God and trusting Him with our pain is always better than running away from Him.
6. Listening to each other is always better than yelling at each other.
7. We need each other. Together we will survive this problem.

WHAT ABOUT YOU?

1. What are your greatest challenges at this point in your marriage?
2. Presently, are the challenges bringing the two of you closer, or driving you apart?
3. What changes do you feel are needed in your marriage?
4. Would you be willing to share your ideas with your spouse?

8

All the Goodbyes: Facing Grief

By the time we're into our "second half," we're well acquainted with loss: with saying goodbye to beloved people (including our own kids), to cherished places, to a regular paycheck, to the energy once taken for granted, to the dreams of youth. We lose friends and jobs and ideals. It can leave us with an aching emptiness.

"My husband and I lost our mothers within four months of each other," one wife said. "There were eerie similarities. They were both longtime widows. They both suffered from dementia. The cause of death was not clear: pneumonia, dehydration, or malnutrition. They both just . . . faded away.

"That was not a good year. But it wasn't so much a wrenching, sobbing grief. We knew that for both of them it was a blessed release. It felt more like emptiness, an unfilled space in your life. And with that came collateral losses, things you don't think about: the house you'll never go in again, the casserole you'll never eat, the trip you'll never take. It was not raw grief but more of a melancholy.

"It made us think how you need to *add*—not just subtract—at this stage of life. You have each other, but even with that, you need your world to be fuller. So we started looking for ways to serve others."

"THESE ARE THE HAPPIEST DAYS OF MY LIFE": A SON AND FATHER RECONCILE

Each person's bereavements are unique. Each marriage is affected in ways intertwined with a lifetime of relationships and experiences. What happens during end-of-life days sometimes opens hearts and renews spirits in unexpected ways. Ask Ted and Linda (the couple on the boat in chapter 1).

Ted's parents divorced after fifty-two years of marriage. He and his sisters spent much more time with their fearful mother than with their angry father. Ted says they were expected to "take sides" against their dad.

"One day my dad chewed me out on the phone," Ted says. "When he took his anger out on me, I thought, 'I'm done with this!' I felt bad, and for three months had no contact with him. Finally I wrote a letter, and then he called me. For the first time *ever* he said, 'I am so sorry.'"

Ted was fifty-one and his dad eighty-six when they began reconciling. One day, while visiting in their home, his father grumbled to Linda about the way he was treated by his family, and started criticizing Ted. "Wait a minute!" she objected, cutting him short. "Let me tell you what's going on."

"That was a turning point," Linda tells us. "He was impressed by a woman standing up to him."

"—but not condemning him," Ted said.

His father had had affairs, and early in their marriage, Ted told Linda that he was worried he would become like his dad. She assured him he wouldn't. "You're not going to be like that. You're loyal, and we're a team."

As his father aged into his nineties, Ted's relationship with his dad improved. He knew his father was a caring person. He had started a program for the handicapped, and Ted thought, *He bailed people out, but no one bailed him out.*

Yet as time passed, Ted desired more healing between them.

When his father was 101, under hospice care, Ted and Linda stayed with him in his apartment. They would put a mattress on the floor of his living room to sleep at night, and often Ted would lie beside his dad on his bed. There had been a long softening in their relationship. When the hospice worker asked his father if he would like a hospital bed brought in, he said, "No. Then my son can't be next to me."

As they and Ted's sister sat with him on the edges of his bed, there was a sense of reconciliation, and remarkably, the dying man told them, "These are the happiest days of my life."

The most profound experience for Ted came a little later. "In one of those moments I pulled my chair next to him, and I put my hand on his head. Suddenly I felt his hand on my head. He held it there for a long while before pulling it away. It was his farewell message to me. It was the blessing from him I had been searching for all my life."

THE LONELINESS OF GRIEF

In grief, many couples naturally turn to each other, and their mutual compassion deepens their bonds. Yet everyone's grief is unique, and sometimes it's hard to see past one's own pain. As we visited with couples who opened up about their losses of loved ones, we were reminded of how differences in the ways we grieve can generate extreme pain and resentments. In particular, the death of a child, or an adult child's spouse, can confuse and isolate even a mature, loving couple.

One spouse may be paralyzed with grief while the other "soldiers on." One may be stumbling in disbelief and anger at God while the other desperately tries to affirm faith. Suddenly, a peaceful marriage is plunged into tempestuous waters.

The pain we saw reminded us of Robert Frost's "Home Burial." In it, the poet laureate reveals the confrontation of a husband and wife who are stricken and bewildered. Frost wrote from personal experience: his firstborn son, Elliot, died at the age of three, and later two more children died. Here are brief excerpts from "Home Burial":

The husband describes the little graveyard behind their home:

"So small the window frames the whole of it . . .
There are three stones of slate and one of marble . . .
    "Don't, don't, don't, don't," she cried.
She withdrew, shrinking from his arm . . .

"Can't a man speak of his own child he's lost?"
"Not you!"

The wife goes on to reveal what she saw:

"If you had any feelings, you that dug
With your own hand—how could you—his little grave;
I saw you from that little window there,
Making the gravel leap and leap in air,
Leap up like that, like that, and land so lightly,
And roll back down the mound beside the hole.
I thought, Who is that man? I didn't know you."

A simple search online will put "Home Burial" on your screen. Why read it? As Frost reveals, when grief comes, wives and husbands can become strangers to each other; sometimes even those of us blessed with stable marriages.

"In bed at night she would often turn her back to me, curl into a tight ball, and cry."

It was at a convention in Nashville that we first talked with David and Nancy Guthrie about the loss of their child. In an open session they shared their experiences and the healing insights they were gleaning from the book of Job. Later, they lost another child, and ever since they have been ministering to other bereaved parents.

In their book, *When Your Family's Lost a Loved One,* they give examples of ways couples grieve differently, and the dark seeds that can grow. In their case, early in their grieving process, they read the story of a bereaved mother who resented her husband's not being as sad as she was. After their son's death, her husband had returned to work, and his apparent lack of grief was creating a chasm between them. Yet when the mother learned that every day on the way to work, he pulled over and wept, she realized they were grieving in different ways. Reading the story warned David and Nancy that their mourning might take different paths that could lead them apart.

Later David wrote, "In the darkest times of her grief, Nancy seemed to curl up inside herself. Since she'd always been such an open person, this was strange and a bit frightening to me. Feeling insecure, I instinctively retreated from her as if I'd been rebuffed. In bed at night she would often turn her back to me, curl into a tight ball, and cry. If I tried to comfort her, I felt her tense and disappear deeper, like an armadillo inside its shell."

David says he determined at those times "to stay close, hold on to her, mostly keep my mouth shut, and just be there."

The late author Joseph Bayly and his wife, Mary Lou, lost, unimaginably, three sons: one after surgery, one from leukemia, another from a sledding accident. In his book he writes that in such times of grief a husband and wife need more love, yet they may find their relationship "severely strained, even deteriorating." He observes that it's different for each spouse, and describes common patterns of withdrawal: "not mentioning the child who died; breakdown of communication; escape into sleep; pulling apart from one another in friendships, especially new ones; and absorption in club or church activities."

Grief is not a single emotion. It is rather a bundle of emotions.

Here is Joe Bayly's counsel for bereaved couples:

"This is the time to close ranks, the time for concern about your partner's affectional and sexual satisfaction, the time to force yourselves to talk to each other and to listen, as if your marriage depended on it. Sometimes it does."

"THEY CAN'T DO THIS TO YOU!"

In the second half of marriage, not all grief is associated with the death of family members. Sometimes there is the loss of a job.

David is the president of a small company where he has worked for twenty-five years. Now, at the age of sixty-one, he walks into his office for an appointment with the CEO of the larger corporation that owns his company. He is told that his services are no longer needed, and that Friday will be his last day. David goes home that evening in shock, and shares with his wife, Sarah, a message she never expected to hear. She is furious, and lashes out in anger toward the man who delivered the news. Then she expresses her frustration toward David. "Are you just going to accept this? This is unfair! You must fight for what is right! They can't do this to you! You've got to stand up to them!"

"There's no use in fighting it," David says. "This happens all the time. Suing the corporation would cost thousands, and it isn't worth the effort." He walks out of the room feeling rejected by his wife, and Sarah goes to the bedroom crying with resentment in her heart toward her husband and the corporation.

David and Sarah have experienced their initial shock to great loss. He is stunned, and she is angry. Grief is not a single emotion. It is rather a bundle of emotions. Shock, fear, anger, resentment, frustration, and numerous other emotions are all a part of what we call grief. Individuals have different emotions at different times, and their response to these emotions will also widely differ. That is why grief often brings withdrawal, separation, and sometimes divorce in a marriage.

After numerous arguments, David and Sarah realized they needed help. Wisely, they reached out to a Christian counselor who helped them understand the process of grief, and that their varied responses to grief need not be divisive. Sarah said, "I feel closer to David now, more than ever. Our marriage had gotten into a rut. We did the same things every week with little time for each other. But his loss of a job pushed me over the edge. Looking back I realize how unfair I was to David, demanding that he correct something that could not be corrected. I'm so glad that we went for counseling. I hate to think what might have happened if we had continued on our course of arguing with each other."

David and Sarah illustrate the importance of seeking help in a time of grief. It may be reaching out to trusted friends, a pastor, or a counselor, but all of us need people when we are going through various stages of grief.

There is no five-step program for processing grief. However, there are common elements that people tend to go through in the face of significant losses in life. Shock is typically the first response, which can be helpful for a short time, but then emotions will, and should be, expressed. We have tear ducts for a reason, and yes, even men need to cry. Depression, loneliness, and isolation are also feelings that will surface during grief. Sometimes there are physical symptoms such as headaches and backaches. Physicians recognize that many physical symptoms are rooted in emotional stress.

Feelings of guilt may also accompany grief as we look back at the loss and begin to blame ourselves for what happened. As noted above, anger and resentment are very common emotions. Withdrawing from the normal routines of life is another typical response of grief. The most fundamental vehicle for processing grief is sharing our thoughts and feelings with others. We do not mean that all conversation should focus on your grief, but we do strongly believe that grief needs to be a shared experience. Those of us who are trying to help people who are processing grief need to understand that when we bring up the subject of their loss, whether it's a job or the death of a family member, we are doing them a great service. We are in essence communicating, "I remember and I care."

"I PACK A BOX AND THEN I CRY"

Another common loss for those of us in the second half of marriage occurs when we physically move from one location to another. Bob and Kathy had lived in the same town and attended the same church for forty years. Basically, all of their married life had been lived in this community. Their three children had moved away and were living scattered across the country. As the two of them began to have some physical problems, they began to discuss their future. As they shared their discussions with their daughter, she and her husband insisted they move to their town where they could take care of them. After much thought and prayer, Bob and Kathy agreed. However, as the time drew near Bob and Kathy began to experience grief. Kathy said, "I pack a box and then I cry. Then later I pack another box and cry again.

In each period of grief we have asked each other, "How may I best help you?" Sometimes the answer has been: "Just hold me."

It is so hard to leave all our friends."

Bob said, "It's the hardest thing we've ever done, but we know it's the right thing. We've met people out there, and know that God will give us new friends. We are so grateful that our daughter and her husband are willing to do this for us." Bob and Kathy are processing their grief in a very positive way by sharing with their friends. They realize that, while they are losing their house and all of their familiar environment, including friends, they are also gaining a sense of security in being near their daughter. They choose to be optimistic about making new friends, and getting involved in a new church. Grief can turn to gain when processed in a healthy manner.

"CONCENTRATE ON THE BIRDS"

Back to our friend at the beginning of the chapter who was wondering about "adding, not just subtracting" in this time of all-too-frequent loss. The "gain" can come in the form of how we see things. One husband put it this way:

"When is a bird larger than a mountain? When it's on your window ledge and the mountain is in the distance. It's all in how we see things. We need to concentrate on the birds and the 'beautiful' in our lives and not allow the mountains to cast cold shadows over us."

All of us will experience grief. I (Gary) have experienced the death of my dad, my mother, and my fifty-eight-year old sister, my only sibling. Karolyn, too, has lost her parents and four siblings. In each period of grief we have asked each other, "How may I best help you?" Sometimes the answer has been: "Just hold me." Other times, "Give me some space." We have learned to respect each other's answers because we know that grief takes many turns on the road to healing.

9

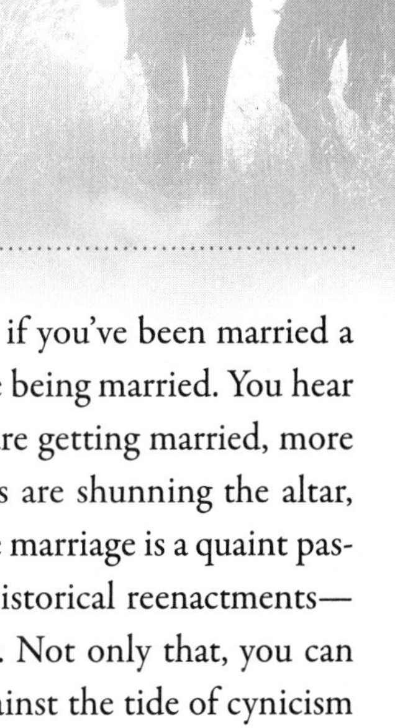

Two Are Better than One

It's easy to feel out of step these days if you've been married a long time *and* if you really, really like being married. You hear the statistics about how fewer people are getting married, more couples are living together, millennials are shunning the altar, and on and on. You can start to feel like marriage is a quaint pastime like knitting or participating in historical reenactments—a curiosity indulged in by a select few. Not only that, you can feel like you're swimming upstream against the tide of cynicism about the viability of lifelong love and commitment. One online article claimed that it's impossible to stay compatible for a lifetime, and a reader responded that traditional marriage "is as dead as the Edsel, marriages flounder and fall like ripe mangoes." He advised, "Don't even think of long-term marriage!"

Is marriage a false dream, bound to shatter hearts? Yes, if it's the fairy-tale stuff of living happily-ever-after in a trouble-free castle. But committing to the long haul in marriage is a call to rugged adventure that just might result in a happy ending. We're hardwired for it.

As mentioned in chapter 2, when Andy and Phyllis tell college students they've been married nearly forty years, applause erupts. Young adults hunger for the vision of long, stable marriages. When they see couples actually enjoying marriage, their spirits rise. Maybe there is hope!

Leaders in many fields now say we desperately need models of healthy marriages and a much greater awareness of how vital marriage is and how good marriage can be. The truth is, such models are all around us, but they are mostly obscure to media and the broader culture. But we know them. They're friends, relatives, coworkers, fellow church attenders. They're clients and neighbors and the nice woman who always checks our vision at the eye doctor.

They're us.

And as we said at the beginning of this book, each of us blessed with a thriving and resilient marriage, with warm companionship and shared jokes, and, yes, a robust physical intimacy, can echo the James 1:17 verse on God's good gifts: "Every good and perfect gift is from above, coming down from the Father of the heavenly lights . . . "

A good marriage is a gift. It is grace: undeserved, unmerited favor. It should humble us every day.

We have talked a great deal in this book about trials and losses and how to thrive when the hard times come. But as we all know, there's a lot more to marriage than trials (thank God). There's the simple *enjoyment* of our mates, day in, day out. Remember the woman with all the pets? She said, "On a recent warm Sunday afternoon, I was feeling really burned out. I'd been working hard and also involved with helping our grown kids. I needed a break. So my husband and I took all our pets, birds, fish, dog, out to our patio. We sat with the Sunday paper and read. There was a really interesting article about how search firms are springing up to help churches find pastors. So we talked about that, and a lot of other things, and drank water with a squirt of lemon but no ice because our icemaker is broken.

"*That* is one of the joys of the second half of marriage. Those moments, one after another after another . . ."

And *that* is what the cynics are missing out on.

"WE FELT LOVED"

Another story.

The gift of the long marriage also comes with, if not a "cast of thousands," many, many dear others whose lives have intertwined with ours over the years. Jeanette and I (Harold) experienced this a few years ago. Well after midnight, we and our three youngest children were sound asleep in our house when a heavy thunderstorm moved in. Lightning struck. Our house caught fire, and smoke alarms went off. Jeanette, roused and seeing fire, yelled to get out of the house. I hustled our kids out of their bedrooms and into the rain outside.

Soon fourteen fire trucks were in our cul-de-sac, and dozens of neighbors stood with us watching our house burn. As we think back to that night and the year that followed, what we remember most are countless acts of kindness:

- Our neighbors in the downpour and darkness bringing us clothes and offering to take us in.
- A city employee coming before dawn to assure me he'd approve reconstruction plans.
- In the morning, friends going to Target for necessities like toothbrushes.
- Neighbors, hearing the day of the fire happened to be our daughter's twelfth birthday, bought and wrapped presents for her.
- People at church signed up to bring meals, help fill the dumpsters in our driveway, and record our scorched possessions for insurance claims. Work colleagues in various ways chipped in to help us.

Yes, we lost precious things in the fire, and we ran flat-out that year to get back to normal. Jeanette supervised the house reconstruction, and I took on the mountains of insurance paperwork, and we both dealt with our kids' school schedules. Yet what we now focus on about that year are the many ways people cared for us.

Jeanette sums it up: "We felt loved."

Gary: A Personal Word

Harold and I have enjoyed the process of interviewing and listening to scores of couples who have shared with us life in the second half of marriage. I want to end with a personal word. My wife, Karolyn, and I are "married and still loving it" for over five decades. We have walked together through sunshine and rain, through darkness and light. We have been open about sharing the struggles of the early years of our marriage. It was in those dark days that I often thought, "I have married the wrong person. This is never going to work, we are too different." I was in seminary at the time studying to be a pastor, and the closer I came to graduation, the more I realized that I could never stand before people and preach a message of hope when I was so miserable in my marriage.

I will never forget the day I finally said to God, "I don't know what else to do. I've done everything I know to do and it is not getting any better." As soon as I prayed that prayer, there came to my mind a visual image of Jesus on His knees, washing the feet of

His followers. And I heard God say to me, "That is the problem in your marriage. You do not have the attitude of Christ toward your wife." It hit me like a ton of bricks because I remembered what Jesus said when He stood up having washed the feet of His disciples: "I am your leader, and in My kingdom this is the way you lead."

I knew that was not my attitude. In the early years my attitude was like, "I know how to have a good marriage. If you will listen to me, we will have one." She would not "listen to me," and I blamed her for our poor marriage. But that day I got a different message. The problem was my own attitude was not Christlike, serving.

So I said to God, "Lord, forgive me. With all of my study in Greek, Hebrew, and theology, I have missed the whole point." Then I said, "Please give me the attitude of Christ toward my wife." In retrospect, it was the greatest prayer I ever prayed regarding my marriage because God changed my attitude.

Three questions made this practical for me. When I was willing to ask these three questions, my marriage radically changed. They are simple questions: 1) What can I do to help you? 2) How can I make your life easier? 3) How can I be a better husband to you? When I was willing to ask those three questions, Karolyn was willing to give me answers. This was long before I knew anything about *The 5 Love Languages*, but essentially she was teaching me how to love her by serving her. When I began to be responsive to her answers, our marriage radically changed. Within three months she started asking me those three questions. We have been walking this road now for a long time, and I have an incredible wife. In fact, not too long ago I said to her,

"If every woman in the world was like you, there would never be a divorce." Why would a man leave a woman who is doing everything she can to help him? And my goal through the years has been to so love and serve my wife that, when I'm gone, she will never find another man to treat her the way I've treated her. She is going to miss me.

If I tried to summarize, I would have to say these are the two essentials: that the husband and wife love and serve each other, thus meeting the emotional need for love and intimacy. And secondly, that they deal effectively with their failures by apologizing and forgiving.

I believe this was God's intention. God never ordained marriage to make people miserable. God ordained marriage because He made us for each other. Two are better than one. God's plan is that we will love and serve each other so that we can then turn, both together and as individuals, and bless the world with the abilities that God has given us.

God used the pain of those early years to give me a deep empathy for people who are struggling with their marriages. When they sit in my office and say, "I have no hope for our marriage," I can honestly say, "I can understand that. So why don't you go on my hope, because I have lots of hope."

I have seen hundreds of couples come to discover the keys to a long-term successful marriage. If I tried to summarize, I would have to say these are the two essentials: that the husband and wife love and serve each other, thus meeting the emotional need for love and intimacy. And secondly, that they deal effectively with their failures by apologizing and forgiving. Apologizing and forgiving are essential because none of us are perfect. Though one man did raise his hand when the speaker asked, "Does anyone know of a perfect husband?" He raised his hand and said loudly, "My wife's first husband." My observation is if there are any perfect husbands, they are deceased. And most of them got perfect after they died.

You do not have to be perfect to have a long-term healthy marriage, but we do have to deal with our failures by apologizing and forgiving.

I have already mentioned the day that our son came home from college, put his right hand on my shoulder and his left hand on Karolyn's shoulder, looked us in the eyes and said, "I want to thank you two for staying together. I have five friends at the university who are not going home this Christmas because their parents have separated and divorced since they left for college. They don't know which parent to visit, so they have decided to stay at the university. I know you guys had lots of trouble in the early years, but I want to thank you for staying together." We embraced and experienced tears of joy that God had helped us, and not only kept us together but gave us a loving, caring, supportive relationship.

It is our desire that the stories you have read in this book, and the principles we have observed in the lives of those who are "Married and Still Loving It," will encourage you to face realistically the joys and challenges of the second half. We sincerely believe that the second half can be the best half. If you have found the book helpful, we hope that you will share it with your friends, and perhaps use it as a foundation for discussion in a study group.

The greatest thing we can do for the marriages of the next generation is to give them a model of a husband and wife who love each other, are deeply committed to each other's well-being, who deal effectively with their failures, and seek to honor God in all they do. We hope that this book will help you do that "so long as you both shall live."

John and Cindy Trent

"LEAN INTO THE FACT THAT JESUS HOLDS OUR FUTURE"

DR. JOHN TRENT *is possibly best known as coauthor, with Gary Smalley, of the bestseller* The Blessing, *as well as introducing the Lion, Otter, Beaver, and Retriever personalities in his and Smalley's book* The Two Sides of Love. *He recently was named as Gary D. Chapman Chair of Marriage and Family Ministry and Therapy at Moody Theological Seminary. He and his wife, Cindy, who teaches English as a Second Language to first- and second-graders, live in Scottsdale, Arizona. They have been married thirty-six years and have two grown daughters, Kari and Laura.*

What does adventure look like for you?

In our marriage, Cindy is a teacher and planner and organizer. Think about Bilbo Baggins in *The Hobbit* who was very content to stay in the Shire and enjoy his Hobbit home in the hill without going on any adventures—ever. Meaning, I quickly learned that hang-gliding or extreme skiing or scuba diving in a shark tank probably weren't things Cindy and I were going to together to build adventure into our marriage.

But we've learned that adventure doesn't have to be life-threatening. In fact, some of what keeps our marriage fresh is the everyday adventure of doing things together that just take us a few steps out of our comfort zone. For example, the two of just started going to an incredibly challenging (to us) workout place right near our home called Orange Theory Fitness. Normally, we are the oldest people in the place by *decades*. Almost every time we gripe, "Why are we doing this?" But it's always fun to just survive a challenging hour-long workout together.

We live in a big city, so we force ourselves to go to a new restaurant every other week instead of the same places we've gone for years. And with our girls gone, we're at a new church (again, as some of the oldest people in the place) and we just started a new Bible study for couples, something we never had time to do with the girls home. So, not "extreme" things. But new things. And we're committed to not shying away from places or experiences that "people our age" don't often do. Even if the music is loud at our new church and other gray heads few and far between.

What do you see as your biggest challenge at this stage of your marriage?

In reading this question, Cindy and I said almost simultaneously, "Keeping our relationship strong with our out-of-state daughters!" So much has changed as both Kari (our older daughter) and Laura (our younger) have moved from our home in Arizona, launched their careers, and now both have been dating young men for almost a year. (As I write this, both men have sat down with me to "have the talk" in the last month!)

We raised both our girls to "go for it!" To follow big dreams and to work hard serving the Lord and others. But the problem is, they took that to heart! That call to "do something great" has included both girls choosing to go on mission trips to challenging places (where we just had to pray and not worry) and finishing graduate school and setting up shop in places they felt the Lord was directing them (places that aren't in the city where we live!). And we urged both to put their expectations on the Lord, not the wedding industry—and wondered at times if they would ever find time to date!

We've seen both girls become outstanding young women who love the Lord and who have jumped head-first into life. But that has included each attending excellent out-of-state schools and having the confidence and vision to move to Seattle and Dallas to pursue their careers. Each a long way from Arizona! So it's keeping that relationship with super-busy kids, with differing schedules and challenges, strong from a distance.

You have an interesting working-and-commuting lifestyle—one that's becoming more common. How did the two of you work all this out?

While the economy has forced many couples into a long-distance commute-to-work lifestyle, travel has been something Cindy and I have had to factor into building and strengthening our marriage for thirty-five years. Early in my ministry I started getting asked to go speak at different places. From the beginning, I thank the Lord we made three decisions that have kept travel from becoming something that pulled us apart emotionally, even if we were apart physically.

First, I let Cindy set my schedule. Meaning, she had a vote on when and where I went. That way I didn't say yes to a trip that erased my being home for a big event for the kids—or for Cindy. She was all in or I didn't get on the plane. I speak a good deal at military bases across the country and world, so I know that many people in the service or workplace do not have the flexibility I do to say no to a great opportunity that doesn't fit in with a greater responsibility at home. But getting Cindy to say yes to a trip before I do has been a decision the Lord has certainly honored.

The second great decision we made early on was that no trip would be a parentheses. Meaning, I sit down with Cindy before each trip and make sure she knows "Here's what I'm doing Monday, here's the place I'm speaking Tuesday . . ." That way my absence isn't just a blank space, but she knows what and who to pray for while I'm away. With the kids, I even got a US map and would show them exactly where I was going, and share what I'd be doing each day.

Finally, I call home a *lot* when on the road. I've met and traveled with many people who won't call home for three of four days on a trip (again, when they've not been deployed and been in cell reception the entire time). That's ridiculous if you're serious about keeping your marriage strong. You're not bothering your spouse with at least daily calls to check in—you're saying, "You matter! Even when I'm on the road!" The absence of a relationship doesn't make a strong relationship.

John, you took on this new position as the Chapman Chair at a time when a lot of boomers are looking toward retirement or at least not jumping into a new professional challenge. Say more about that.

Chuck Swindoll has been a friend and mentor (at a distance) for years. I heard him say and saw him model that attitude was everything when it came to aging. "Have this attitude in yourself" is a biblical blueprint, I think, for staying ready for a challenge to serve others. Any time, any age.

I was recently given the incredible honor of being named the first Gary D. Chapman Chair of Marriage and

Family Ministry at Moody Theological Seminary. It's perhaps the most fun and challenging opportunity I've ever taken on. But I never looked at it as an age thing. Meaning, just because I'm on the older side of the ledger, I think about it as an attitude thing. Like Caleb said to Joshua, "Give me the hill country!" (Joshua 14:12)—the toughest territory to tackle. The family is under attack from all sides in ways that few could have imagined even a decade ago. It's an honor to get to step into the battle and seek to train the next generation of family ministers and counselors to stand alongside God's people in these challenging days. And no, I'm not going to dye my hair at this stage of the game, or dress any differently. That's not the key to fitting in. The key is serving your way into being someone the Lord can use in that position He's opened before you—not sitting back and saying to yourself you're too old to be there.

How would you counsel a couple whose millennial kids seem uncertain about/skeptical of marriage? How do we encourage them without being overinvolved?

Many millennial kids are pushing back the age at which they marry (or even date), or they're even questioning whether marriage is a viable option these days. It's not easy to sit back as a parent and not push a child to get moving in terms of meeting someone and moving toward marriage. We've had the conversations with our girls about online dating as an option and being open to going on one date with someone who asks them out and fits their parameters. But for most parents, trying to push a child toward marriage is like pushing a rope. You have very little leverage—outside of prayer and encouragement. One of the best things we did was encourage our girls to continually realize the marriage industry creates a constant craving for something that isn't really what's best for a person. We urge them to date and be open to marriage, but not be pushed into a wedding when the issue is a lifetime marriage with someone who loves and serves the Lord.

Psychologically and spiritually, how do you deal with anxiety about the future, and what would you advise other second-half couples?

Cindy grew up in an alcoholic home with incredible insecurity and tension. I grew up in a single-parent home where the money often didn't stretch to the end of the month. Both of us look to Jesus to be our source of security for the future—but we've also had to struggle in different ways with anxiety about the future. And I don't think we're alone. I meet *many* couples who worry about health, finances, and a world filled with changes and challenges. What I'd advise couples our age is to really lean into the fact that Jesus holds our future. He never leaves us alone to face aging, or illness, or 401ks shrinking, or watch friends' health or fortunes declining or prove inadequate. Rather, grab hold of verses like Hebrews 13:5: "For He Himself has said, 'I will never leave you nor forsake you'" (NKJV). While the future can seem and be uncertain, we are not walking into it alone. Not for an instant.

And the second way of facing anxiety for me comes from realizing *actions* dictate feeling, not the reverse. If we're feeling anxious, we're not going to move past the stress or fear we're experiencing by waiting for our feelings to change! ACTIONS DICTATE FEELINGS. Meaning it's when we take steps to plan a budget, or eat better, or exercise more often, or step into serving together as a couple instead of sitting—our actions are what change our feelings. And this leads right into the next question.

How can a husband and wife bless each other?

There is a tremendous verse that I think outlines what it means to bless our spouse—at any age and stage. Deuteronomy 30:19 was a challenge God set before His people as they were ready to take their first steps into the Promised Land. "Today I have given you the choice between life and death, between blessings and curses. Now I call on heaven and earth to witness the choice you make. Oh, that you would choose life, so that you and your descendants might live!" (NLT).

To me, a quick look at those four words, life and death, blessing and curse, lay out a clear path for couples our age, or any age. First, we're to *choose life*. Of course, that means first and foremost we're to choose the source of life: Jesus! He is Life. But that word *life* literally means, "To get moving toward something—someone." So we're to get moving toward the Lord first, who then gets us moving toward our spouse and others. But there is that other choice—death. Which literally means "stepping away" from someone.

But what do we do when we "step toward" others, animated by His life in us?

We're to bless, not curse. The word *bless* in Scripture carries two pictures—one "to bow the knee" and the other "to add weight and value," like adding a coin to a scale. Can you see the connection between those two pictures? Because that person in our life (the Lord, our spouse) is so valuable to us we're to *add* to their life! With our touch, our spoken words, and our genuine commitment. As Dr. Chapman has illustrated so well, we're to use the *life* God's given us to get moving and add those five things that match our loved one's love language. We do this instead of "cursing," which literally means, "to dam up the stream"—to subtract.

So choosing life and blessing gets and keeps us moving toward our spouse and looking for ways to *add* to their life, and keeps us from stepping away from them and seeing our relationship begin to die, or choosing to subtract from our loved one, instead of adding the blessings God would have us add to their life.

For more practical ways of doing this, I just wrote the short books *30 Ways a Husband Can Bless His Wife* and *30 Ways a Wife Can Bless Her Husband*.

Notes

1. Paul Tournier, *The Adventure of Living* (New York: Harper & Row, 1967), 137.

2. Jerry and Shirley Rose, *Significant Living* (New Kensington, PA: Whitaker House, 2000), 15.

3. Gary Chapman, *Now You're Speaking My Language* (Nashville: B&H Books, 2007), 141.

4. For additional help in relating to adult children, see *How to Really Love Your Adult Child* by Gary Chapman, PhD and Ross Campbell, MD (Chicago: Northfield).

5. John 16:33.

6. George Sweeting, *Who Said That?* (Chicago: Moody, 1995), 250.

7. www.healthywomen.org/content/article/sex-after-50, 2.

8. www.psychologytoday.com/blog/all-about-sex/201205/erection-changes-after-50.

Acknowledgments

From Gary:

We would like to thank the many couples who shared with us their personal joys and challenges of the second half. Their stories added the personal touch to what we have written.

We are especially grateful to Jerry and Dianna Jenkins, Joni and Ken Tada, and John and Cindy Trent for taking time to share their journey.

From Harold:

Many thanks to the Moody Publishers team for their strong belief in this book, with special appreciation to Zack Williamson for suggesting the title, John Hinkley for navigating publishing dynamics, and most of all to Betsey Newenhuyse for her full engagement in the conceptual and developmental journey!